WEAVING IRIDESCENCE

COLOR PLAY FOR THE HANDWEAVER

Bobbie Irwin

STACKPOLE
BOOKS

Guilford, Connecticut

Published by Stackpole Books
An imprint of Globe Pequot
Trade Division of The Rowman & Littlefield Publishing
Group, Inc.
4501 Forbes Boulevard, Suite 200, Lanham, Maryland 20706
StackpoleBooks.com

Distributed by
NATIONAL BOOK NETWORK
800-462-6420

British Library Cataloguing in Publication Information
available

Library of Congress Cataloging-in-Publication Data

Names: Irwin, Bobbie, author.
Title: Weaving iridescence : color play for the handweaver /
    Bobbie Irwin.
Description: First edition. | Lanham : Stackpole, 2017.
Identifiers: LCCN 2017018884 (print) | LCCN 2017019279
    (ebook) | ISBN 9780811765800 (e-book) | ISBN
    9780811716284 (pbk. : alk. paper)
Subjects: LCSH: Hand weaving--Patterns. | Color in textile
    crafts. | Iridescence.
Classification: LCC TT848 (ebook) | LCC TT848 .I79 2017
    (print) | DDC 746.1/4--dc23
LC record available at https://lccn.loc.gov/2017018884

First Edition

Printed in the United States of America

♾™ The paper used in this publication meets the minimum
requirements of American National Standard for Information
Sciences—Permanence of Paper for Printed Library Materials,
ANSI/NISO Z39.48-1992.

CONTENTS

ACKNOWLEDGMENTS

This book would not have happened without the inspiration, encouragement, and insistence of so many people who have attended my lectures and workshops. Some of the classes turned into brainstorming sessions that sent me home excited to try new experiments. I'm indebted to those weavers and other friends who asked intriguing questions, introduced me to different perspectives, shared references, provided wonderful samples, gave excellent advice and technical assistance, and asked me to write a book about iridescence.

Special thanks go to my friends at Stackpole Books, especially my editors. Debra Smith's enthusiasm about my topic helped convince the company to offer me a publishing agreement. While I was writing, I much appreciated her confidence in my ability to undertake this project, as well as her calm reassurance whenever I was feeling overwhelmed. I'm also grateful to Candi Derr, who expertly coordinated revisions between me and other editors and designers to make my words flow smoothly and turn my manuscript into a book.

A number of weavers from around the world generously shared photographs and samples for me to include here. Their expertise, innovations, and equipment exceed my own, and I am delighted to be able to include examples of their beautiful and inspiring work. Thanks, especially, go to Cynthia Broughton, Judy Hanninen, Agnes Hauptli, Bonnie Inouye, Wendy Morris, Barbara Setsu Pickett, Marian Stubenitsky, and Susan Wilson.

As always, I much appreciate the support and technical assistance of my husband, Reed Irwin. As well as patiently handling the stress and general disruptions that are involved when I create a book, he willingly took on the daunting task of photographing these challenging textiles with considerable persistence and skill.

I've been interested in science since I was a child, and research has always been a joy. After discovering weaving while finishing my master's thesis in geology, I started applying the scientific research skills I'd learned to my new focus on textiles.

Periodically, I've had a question about some aspect of weaving or spinning that I wanted to know more about, something that had not been published extensively. I especially like to study this sort of topic so that I can form and test my own theories and come to my own conclusions without being overly influenced by someone else's work. Good research never ends, but most of my research projects have lasted a couple of years, until I've felt confident enough to write about them and teach them. Of all my studies, nothing else has captured my interest to the same extent as iridescence, and I'm still learning.

There has been surprisingly little information in popular books and magazines about iridescence in textiles, even though weavers have been creating these magical fabrics deliberately for centuries. This book is intended to help fill that void and is the result of more than a dozen years of study and teaching. This is not a typical step-by-step craft book, although there are some projects for readers who prefer specific instructions. It is intended as a comprehensive (but not exhaustive) guide to the many factors involved in designing fabrics with successful iridescence, and I hope you will be inspired to try your own experiments with this fascinating subject.

Because I don't work easily with color, many years ago I decided to weave a large color sampler so I'd have a visual reference of what happens when I cross threads of different colors. I wasn't looking for iridescence and didn't notice it with the matte yarns I chose, although now I can find it in my sampler. I did notice that some combinations appeared to vibrate, as though my eyes couldn't decide which color to concentrate on. I later learned that these combinations tend to be iridescent.

The big lesson I learned from this project was that there were two colors that seemed to work well with every other color with which I crossed them. These were colors I rarely, if ever, used. One, magenta, I didn't mind; the other, chartreuse, was one I'd always disliked and avoided. However, I liked what happened when they were placed in company with other colors, and so to push myself out of my comfort zone, over the years I deliberately incorporated one or the other in my weaving. When I signed up for an international napkin/serviette exchange in 2002, I decided to include *both* red-violet and yellow-green in my napkins, and, thinking this was an odd combination, I decided to weave some samples first. What happened was iridescence.

"Sometimes it just happens" was one weaver's comment as part of an Internet group discussion about weaving iridescent fabrics. I understood. The color effect I discovered while sampling for napkins was a pleasant surprise and not something I'd planned, and it sparked my interest in studying iridescence. However, my background as a scientist told me there were reasons for the phenomenon, and I wanted to understand and control it so I could design iridescent fabrics with confidence. I'm sharing my studies in this book so that you can do the same.

What Is Iridescence?

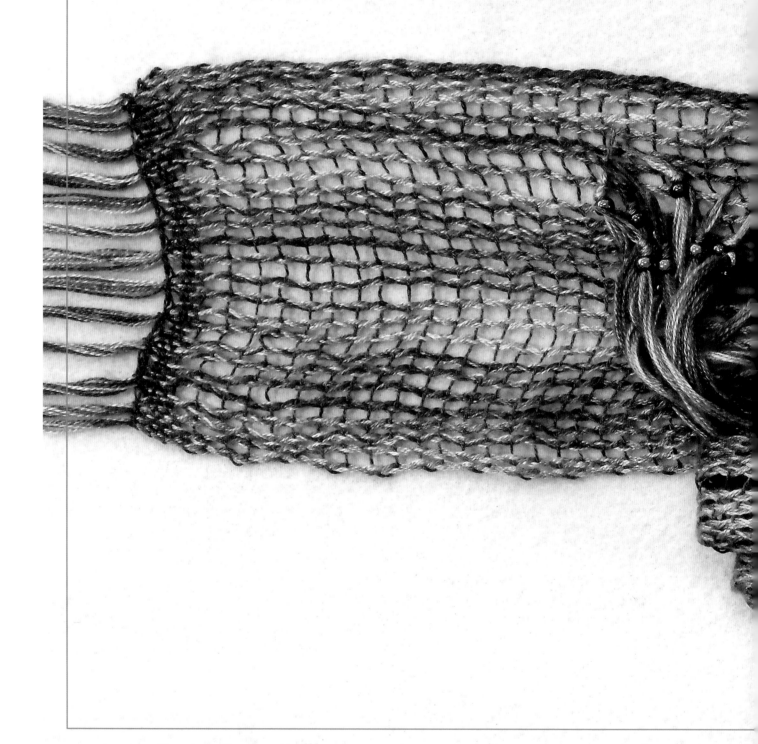

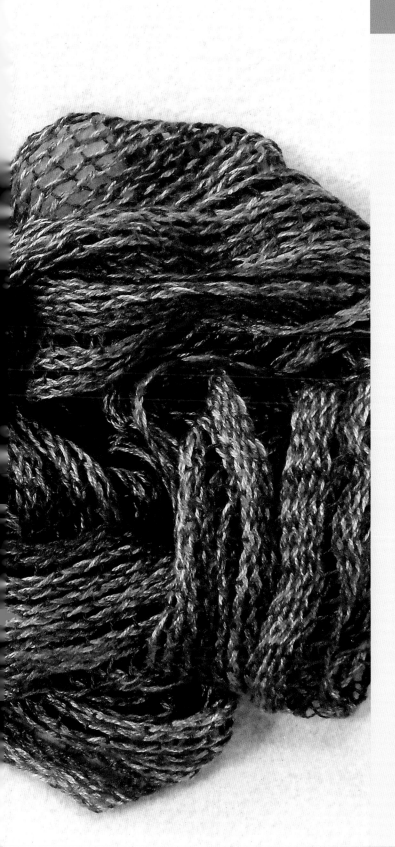

ridescence is an apparent change in color as the angle of view changes or, as one dictionary defines it, "a play of colors." That's a description I particularly like, since I have had great fun playing with colors since I started my study!

Many man-made materials these days are designed to be iridescent, often showing a wide range of colors at any particular angle. These include everything from gift wrap and notebook covers to sequins, beads, plastics, and glass, and their effects usually mimic the multicolored iridescence in some natural objects. Raku pottery, certain ceramic glazes, and tarnished or treated metal can also be iridescent. Compact discs for computers display an iridescent rainbow. Iridescent effects and substances can even be printed onto fabrics!

Natural Iridescence

Iridescence in natural objects can show a spectrum of colors, as on an oil slick or a soap bubble, or a single bright color, as in many feathers. In a sense, most iridescence in natural objects is an illusion because the colors are not an inherent part of the object but rather the effect of light entering the substance and interacting with its structure. Even the iridescent "eye" of a peacock feather, which does not appear to shift, is the result of the physics of light when it encounters the microscopic aspects of the feather.

Iridescence is incorporated into many man-made items, such as this "carnival glass" bowl and these plastic grapes.

Many natural objects exhibit iridescence, such as these minerals (bornite and opal).

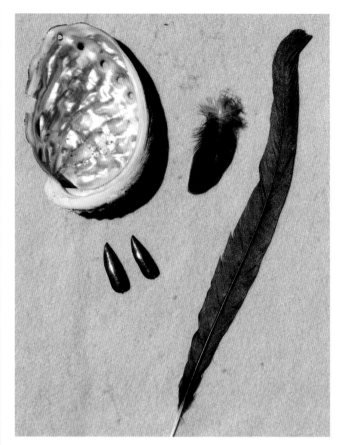

Insect parts (here, beetle wings), shells, and feathers can also be iridescent.

Many naturally iridescent objects, such as certain feathers, shells, and fish scales, are drab colors until we see light reflected from them at a particular angle. Oil slicks and soap bubbles are colorless but can appear banded with many colors. Some layered insect wings and minerals also exhibit iridescence. Natural iridescence is typically a brilliant, almost metallic color effect.

Iridescence in Fabric

An iridescent fabric is (in most cases) one that appears to change color as your angle of view changes. Moving or crumpling a fabric helps you see it at different angles and enhances the iridescent effect. Color shifts are particularly evident viewed at low or steep angles. While iridescence in woven fabric is usually the result of crossing threads of distinct colors, there are also other ways to achieve it. Even so, a fabric must contain, or reflect, more than one color in order to be iridescent. Many iridescent fabrics contain only two colors that intersect at right angles (warp and weft), and I will refer to that as *traditional* iridescence.

There is another definition of iridescence in fabric to consider. Some people strive for a multicolored effect similar to the spectrum of certain substances with natural iridescence, and there are several ways to accomplish this. Some of these fabrics do have traditional color shifting, at least in part. Others have a more static effect, with multiple colors blending into each other, but lacking a shift with movement. This, too, is true of some natural substances.

We deliberately put colored threads into our fabrics (technically, yarns that will reflect particular colors), and apparent color changes are the result of light reflection from ridges and valleys in the cloth and, sometimes, of color mixing. Light passing through sheer fabrics can give some special effects. Because fabric iridescence is primarily the result of reflection, it is simpler than most natural iridescence.

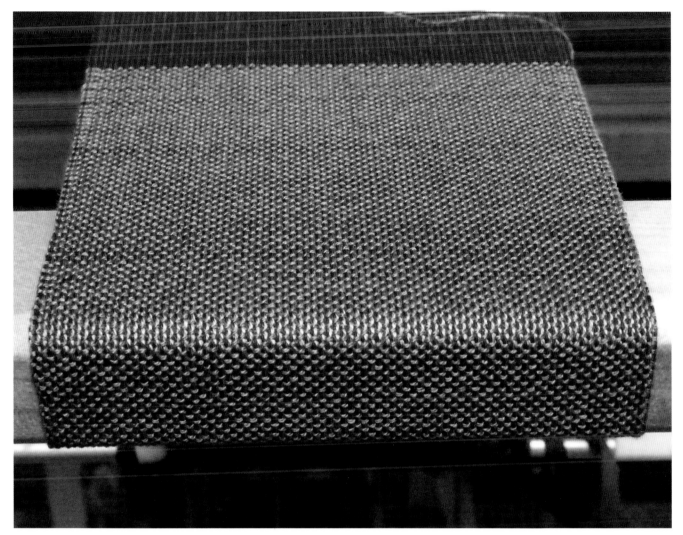

On the loom, an iridescent fabric often shows a bright streak of the warp color as it changes angle going around the breast beam under tension, as if you had woven in a contrasting stripe.

There are lots of "-escence" words, some of which have no relation to color or light. Some of the following light-related terms are erroneously used interchangeably, so it's helpful to understand the differences.

Iridescence: an apparent change of color as the angle of view changes

Opalescence: iridescence with pastel colors, or a play of colors like those in milky opal

Pearlescence: having a pearly luster or sheen

Thermoluminescence: light emitted as the result of heating

Incandescence: glowing associated with intense heat

Luminescence: the emission of cold light energy from atoms

Photoluminescence: luminescence as the result of excitation by light

Fluorescence: the emission of visible colors under ultraviolet light, particularly in certain minerals and chemicals

Phosphorescence: a glow that continues after a light source is removed, from electrons that escape from atoms and don't return immediately

Understanding Optics and Color

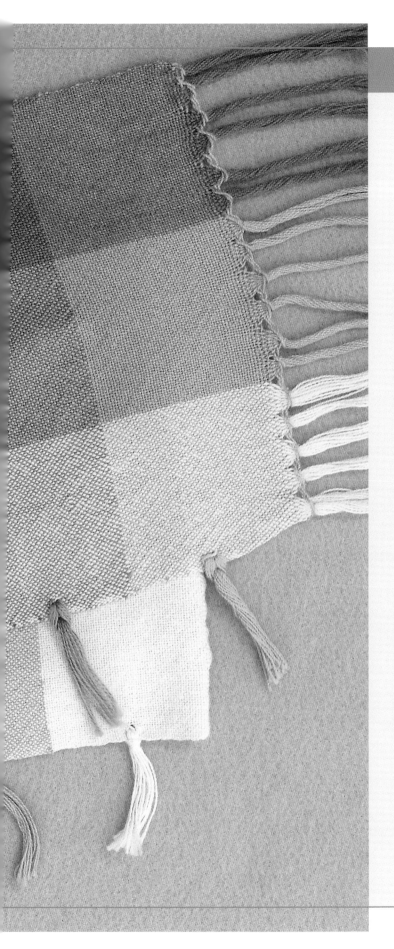

Optics, the science of vision and visible light, including color, is a complex branch of physics that can require years of study to master. Fortunately, it's easy to weave beautiful iridescent fabrics without being an expert in optics. However, a basic knowledge of optics and color theory can help you plan pleasing color combinations with good iridescence and can help you understand why you might get disappointing or unexpected results from time to time.

The Nature of Light

Light and other forms of radiation are disturbances in electrical and magnetic fields, essentially energy that travels in waves with *crests* (high points) and *troughs* (low points), like ripples in water. Scientists identify specific *wavelengths* for this radiation, the distance between one crest or trough and the next. Wavelengths can vary from smaller than the size of an atom to hundreds of miles. The spectrum of electromagnetic radiation includes gamma rays, x-rays, ultraviolet light, visible light, infrared light, microwaves, radio waves, and sound waves, in order of increasing wavelength. Most of these waves are invisible to humans. Visible light is only a tiny part of this spectrum.

Light interacts with substances it enters or passes through. Some light is *transmitted*, as when it passes through clear or translucent objects. When white light passes through a prism or beveled glass,

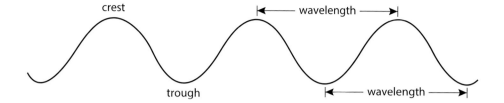

crest

wavelength

trough

wavelength

Wavelength is the distance between one crest or trough and the next.

it is *refracted*, or bent, and it shows a familiar spectrum of colors because the various wavelengths are *dispersed*, or spread out. Shorter violet wavelengths are dispersed more than longer red wavelengths, with the other colors intermediate. A color is not just a specific wavelength; it's associated with a limited range of wavelengths. The color bands we see are of different widths because there is a broader range of wavelengths associated with some colors than with others.

Many objects absorb certain wavelengths of light and *reflect* others, bouncing them back to our vision. Because we see only the reflected colors, you may hear that a substance that appears red, for example, is actually every color *except* red, the color/wavelength that the object "rejects." Since that's confusing, we call it *red*! Brilliant reflection from a shiny surface can look white and may disguise colors that are evident at a different angle of view. Everything we see is the result of reflected light reaching our eyes.

Diffusion is the scattering of light. Some textured objects don't reflect light in a uniform manner.

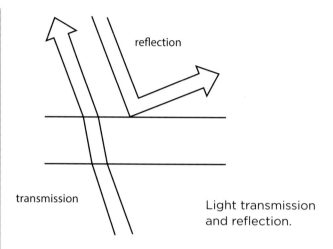

reflection

transmission

Light transmission and reflection.

Light can be subject to *wave interference* when it is reflected from microscopic layers in an object. Some wavelengths of light penetrate deeper than others, and the combined reflections can be unsynchronized. When wave crests coincide, light and color are intensified. When waves are less aligned, colors are less brilliant. When a

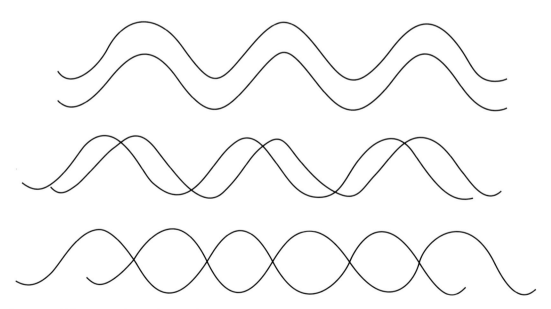

Wave interference: When crests and troughs coincide (top), colors are brilliant. When waves are not synchronized (middle), colors can appear less bright. When troughs mix with crests (bottom), colors are canceled out.

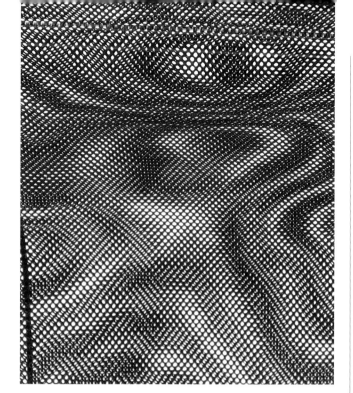
Overlapping grids produce a moiré effect.

trough combines with a crest, colors are canceled out, and you may see only a band of darkness.

Light passing through a very narrow opening—a slot or a grid, like a microscopic screen—can be *diffracted*, or spread, so we detect different colors. The tiny spaces are called a *diffraction grating*. A *reflection grating*, microscopic parallel ridges instead of spaces, can act similarly. On a larger scale, grids or sets of parallel spaces that overlap but are not perfectly aligned create a phenomenon called the *moiré effect*, parallel or concentric bands of dark lines or curves that appear to move as your point of view changes.

Natural iridescence is the result of a variety of light interactions. Many objects with natural iridescence are actually colorless, white, gray, black, or brown and only show brilliant colors when light is reflected from them at certain angles. Refraction, dispersion, and reflection from water droplets create the bands of color in a rainbow, considered to be an example of iridescence. The spectral colors and dark bands on a thin film of oil or soap are the result of wave interference. Tiny ridges or openings in a peacock feather, acting as a reflection or diffraction grating, produce the blue and green "eyes" in what would otherwise be a brown feather.

Precious opal shows a rainbow of colors because it contains layers of tiny spheres that reflect light in multiple directions, and reflection from the layers creates some wave interference. Other iridescent minerals and shells with mother-of-pearl, as well as the layered scales of some fish and of certain insects, owe their brilliant hues to similar optical effects.

How We See

Our eyes contain specialized cells, called *rods* and *cones*, which are sensitive to light and color and transmit that

Iridescence in a peacock feather is the result of complex light interactions.

information to the brain through the optic nerves. Cone cells are stimulated by colors. Rod cells help us see in dim light and aren't sensitive to color. A reduction in the amount of light entering the eye grays colors when the rod cells are more stimulated than the cone cells. Three types of cone cells, sensitive to ranges of short, medium, and long wavelengths of light, transmit information about color that is interpreted by the brain. In a sense, we "see" everything with our brains.

Certain visual abnormalities can affect our perception of color. Some people lack one or more types of cone cells, or their cone cells don't function normally, resulting in varying degrees of *color blindness* or *color deficiency*. This makes it difficult to detect the differences between certain colors (most often red and green), particularly in combination with each other. Some people with color deficiency can distinguish the individual colors, although what they see may be different from the same colors seen by those with normal vision. Someone with red/green deficiency who can still identify reds and greens may not be able to see iridescence in a fabric of red threads crossed with green ones, a color shift that is dramatic to someone with normal vision. This seems especially true if the colors are similar in *value* (relative lightness) and the fabric is woven in close and balanced plain weave, the closest textile interlacement, which produces dots of color. A dark/light color shift may be apparent if the values are different.

The lenses of our eyes yellow with age and absorb more blue light, reducing the amount of blue we see and making colors appear more yellow. A cataract, a clouding of the lens, reduces the amount of light entering the eye and grays color perception.

The eye's lens also filters out ultraviolet light. Before the advent of laser surgery, cataract surgery required the removal of the lens, allowing a person to see some ultraviolet (UV) light that is not normally visible. However, because glass also filters out some ultraviolet light, the thick eyeglasses formerly needed after surgery would act as a UV filter. Modern eye surgery replaces the natural lens with an artificial one.

Understanding Color

Some people seem to have a natural sense of color, automatically knowing how to combine colors for desired effects. Others acquire this skill through considerable study and experimentation. Then there are those of us who struggle with color relationships, even after studying color theory.

There are many books about color, and a few of them relate to fibers and textiles. Most books about color and color theory have been written by artists trained as painters, who work with pigments. It's only possible in this space to give an overview of color theory. The more you study books in detail and actually work with colored materials, the more you can learn about color relationships. There are also excellent references on the Internet.

Color is a subjective topic because nobody knows exactly what someone else sees, and we may see nuances of color differently. Is a particular blue-green more blue

This faceted glass "gem" looks purple in sunlight but switches to blue under fluorescent lights.

I put tassels of the weft yarns on my color samplers and leave warp fringe so I have a quick visual reference of what colors I've used.

or more green? It depends on the viewer. Colors change as the nature of light changes; sunlight near the horizon passes through more pollutants and is redder than it appears overhead in a clear sky. Artificial lighting is usually more yellow or more blue than sunlight. However, an iridescent fabric will still be iridescent under different light conditions, even though the apparent colors may change a bit.

Colors are relative, appearing to change in proximity to each other. When you cross threads of different colors, it can be remarkably difficult to tell which colors you've used unless you keep good records. For example, certain blue and pink yarns that look pleasant side by side change when crossed with each other: the blue might look more violet and the pink goes orange, and the finished effect may not be what you anticipated.

||||||||||||||||||||||||||||||||||||||||||||||||||||||||||||

Q. If you take an iridescent fabric into a dark closet, is it still iridescent?

A. No (because iridescence requires light), but the fabric will still have a lot of potential!

The nature of the light itself can cause colors to change. Colors in shadow look much darker than in bright light. So the color of a green object isn't constant, but the object retains the essence of green.

Colors are defined as narrow ranges of wavelengths, over which people can usually agree they see a particular hue. We see thousands of colors that are not part of a natural spectrum (even though they occur in nature), such as brown, pink, grayish blue, mauve, and olive.

Colors are often categorized by *temperature*, how warm or cool they appear, and our perception varies depending on the light and the proximity of other colors. Violet, blue, green, and intermediate colors are considered cool; they appear to recede when placed next to warm colors of yellow, orange, and red. However, within a particular hue, variations can be considered warm or cool.

Blue is the coolest color, so it would seem that any variation toward green or violet should be warmer. Painters consider a warm blue to have more violet in it and a cool blue to have more green. However, many people sense turquoise (blue-green) as warmer than blue-violet, and since blue is equidistant on a color wheel between the warm colors of yellow and red, labeling a blue *warm* or *cool* is confusing. Similarly, orange is the warmest color. Like blue, it's equidistant from both red and yellow and from violet and green, and labeling its temperature can be confusing.

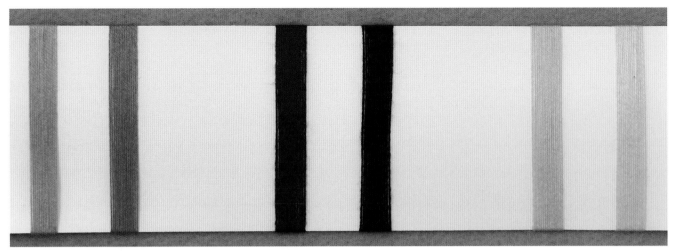

A painter will say the blue on the left (closer to violet) is warmer, while many people not trained as artists will choose the blue on the right (closer to green) as the warmer color.

It helps to know that temperature is often expressed as a relative aspect, in comparison to another color. A single color can appear warmer or cooler depending on a color that surrounds it. If the surrounding color is warmer, the color in question looks cooler. If the surrounding color is cooler, the same color appears warmer. This phenomenon is called *simultaneous contrast*. A color set against a white, gray, or black background will also look different.

Red-violet and yellow-green are intermediate between warm and cool colors. They are particularly useful because they can warm up a cool palette or cool down a warm one.

In these sets of colors (green, red, and yellow), the one on the left of each pair is considered warmer than the one on the right.

Saturation, also called *intensity* by painters (but not by physicists), or *chroma*, is a measure of color purity. A saturated color is neither diluted by white nor darkened by black.

Value, relative lightness or darkness of colors, is an important aspect. From a distance, it's the characteristic we recognize even before we notice color. Paler colors (*tints*) have more white in them and appear lighter than colors combined with black (*shades*). The term *shade* is often misused to refer to any variation of a color, but despite the old Procol Harum song, there's no such thing as a "whiter shade of pale"! The saturated colors in the natural spectrum also have different values: Saturated yellow has the lightest value and saturated violet the darkest, with other colors intermediate in value. A shade of yellow looks like olive and can be darker (of lower value) than a light tint of violet.

Value is one of the easiest color relationships to judge, but our perception can be deceptive. Squinting at two colors reduces the amount of light entering our eyes and helps us judge relative value by making the colors appear more gray. Viewing colors through red plastic also reduces the perception of color, creating a gray scale that makes value comparisons easier. Looking through a translucent black fabric can have a similar effect. Since the red filter is less effective with red objects, a green filter is used for those. These filters, as well as gray-scale cards, are available from some quilt- and art-supply companies. Some smartphones let you take black-and-white images for quick value judgments. Printing a black-and-white copy of colored yarns is a quick and inexpensive way to determine value.

The yellow-green in each combination is the same yarn. Surrounded by blue, it looks warmer; enclosed by orange, it looks cooler. Compared to the highest value, white, it looks darker, and it looks more brilliant next to black. The gray is of similar value (relative lightness) and does not have a distinct influence on the yellow-green.

Combining colors of different values may require smaller amounts of a lighter color in order to keep it from overwhelming a darker color. This effect is easier to achieve when mixing paints than when working with yarn.

Hue is often used as a synonym of *color*, but it can be more strictly defined as a saturated color. *Hue families* include all color variations that can be identified as related to a specific hue. Although popular names such as hunter green, sky blue, and fuchsia mean different things to different people, they help us categorize variations in a hue family.

Black, white, and grays that are mixes only of black and white are technically not colors, but we treat them as colors in our weaving. White light contains all colors, and black, which absorbs all colors, is often said to be the absence of color. *Tones* combine a color with a gray of its same value or result from mixing complements.

In addition to black, white, and gray, other colors are often considered *neutrals*. This includes many pale colors (with light values), plus browns and tans. These can all create iridescence in combination with other colors.

A sampler I wove has brown warps ranging from pale tan to dark brown. The warp colors include warm red-browns, cooler greenish brown (khaki), and gray-brown (taupe). The influence of these components creates some attractive combinations with other colors and contributes to the iridescence. The same is true of many gray yarns, which often contain aspects of other colors. Few

Which color is lighter (of higher value)? A black-and-white copy shows their values are similar; the blue has a slightly higher value.

commercial gray yarns are composed only of white and black; many show the influence of component colors, and even true black is unusual in a yarn.

Color Systems

There are different systems designed to address color relationships, and there is not always agreement over the components and nomenclature, even within the same system. Many of these color systems are based on a circle. All are, to some extent, artificial ways of expressing color, and we can see many thousands more color variations than the strict boundaries a color system allows. A color system is an imperfect but very useful tool to help us understand color.

The *natural spectrum* of a rainbow is often said to have seven colors: red, orange, yellow, green, blue, indigo, and violet. These are the same colors in white light refracted by a prism. Indigo, intermediate between blue and violet, is hard for most people to distinguish, and may have been added to make the "lucky" number seven, in harmony with the seven tones of a (western) musical scale. Physicists and some artists do not consider violet to be part of the natural spectrum, although I can see violet and can't pick out indigo. So according to your preference, the natural spectrum may contain five, six, or seven colors.

Those who work strictly with light use a three-color wheel with *primaries* of blue, green, and red (blue-violet, green, and red-orange according to some sources). Combine these three lights, and you get white light. Green and red light, combined, make yellow; add blue and green to make cyan, and red and blue to make magenta. These resulting mixes are called *secondary* colors. Mix a

primary with the secondary color farthest away from it on the wheel, called its *complement,* and you get white light because the complement is a mix of the other two primaries. Colors that mix to form white light are called *additive.*

Printers use a color wheel with the three primaries that can be combined in ink to create other colors. The primaries are magenta, cyan, and yellow. These combine to make black, a *subtractive* mix. Pigments in inks and dyes are subtractive since they absorb color.

Herbert Ives (1882–1953), an expert in optics and color photography and a television pioneer, devised a 24-color wheel with three "pure" colors: yellow, magenta, and turquoise. This system is the basis of many fabric dyes, and the Ives wheel is popular with quilters, so it is used frequently with textiles.

In the early 1900s, artist Albert Munsell devised his own system as a three-dimensional representation ("color tree") that takes into consideration not only color, but saturation and value. This is a complex system that tries to balance the influence of these factors. It is used by some painters and dyers. The Munsell system has five primaries: red, yellow, blue, green, and purple. (Purple and violet are not always synonymous; artists consider purple to be closer to red, and violet to be closer to blue.)

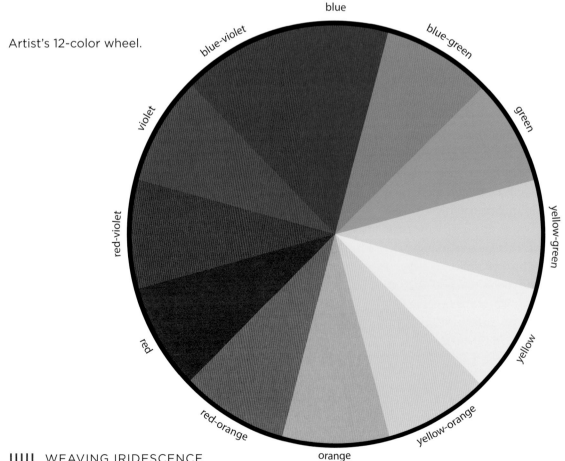

Artist's 12-color wheel.

These yarns, all 10/2 pearl cotton from the same company, show a wide range of blue-greens.

The most common color system used by painters and weavers is an artist's color wheel with 12 colors, and it's the one I use in this book. When artists mix paints, they can't then separate them to return to the original colors. Mixing colors in woven fabrics is different, because we can separate the component threads. However, weavers can achieve some visual effects that are similar to those from mixing paints.

As with other systems, the divisions between the colors are somewhat artificial, and there are no strict dividing lines between adjacent color families—one color grades into another. There is not just one blue-green, as shown on the artist's wheel; the gradations between pure blue and pure green include many colors. In fact, there are two common variations of the 12-color wheel, one using turquoise/cyan to represent blue-green, the other using a greener ("teal") color.

In this system, the primary colors are red, blue, and yellow, which cannot be created by combining other colors. Secondary colors, violet, green, and orange, are mixes of two primaries. *Tertiary* colors combine a secondary color with a primary: blue-violet, red-violet, red-orange, yellow-orange, yellow-green, and blue-green.

Colors that are opposite on the color wheel—as far apart and as different as possible—are called *comple-ments*. A color has two *split complements*, the colors to each side of its complement. Three colors equidistant on the wheel are called a *triad*; lines connecting the three

"pie slices" form an equilateral triangle. Any two pairs of complements will form a *tetrad*, represented by either a square or a rectangle. Tetrads consist of pairs of complements and also include color combinations that are more closely related.

The term *analogous* has differing definitions and refers to closely related colors on the wheel. Some people restrict the term to colors that are side by side, such as red and red-violet; others include colors that are close to each other, such as blue and green. Two, three, or more colors can be considered analogous. Colors within the same hue family, such as a variety of blue-greens, are also analogous. A less useful definition broadens the color range to include five adjacent colors, including two primaries, such as blue, blue-green, green, yellow-green, and yellow. In this book, I use the term *analogous* to mean colors within a three-segment section of the wheel, such as violet, red-violet, and red.

There are other aspects of color relationships that can be helpful in designing attractive fabrics. Artists speak of assortments of colors based on relative value that have major and minor *keys*, as in music: bright combinations or somber or muted ones. Other color combinations based on complements, split complements, and other color-wheel aspects and a limited range of values create color *harmonies*, which may be valuable when working with multicolor iridescence. There are also many other color wheels and color systems to refer to.

Exploring Common Beliefs about Iridescence

Written descriptions of iridescent cloth from as early as the seventh century and paintings by early artists that feature iridescent clothing show that weavers have been creating these magical fabrics deliberately for hundreds of years, but apparently they haven't recorded much information about them. Some of the details may have been trade secrets. A search of popular weaving literature yields some references to iridescent projects but remarkably few details about why iridescence happens or how to design and weave iridescent fabric in general. Much of the information that has been passed along in print or by word of mouth is incomplete, mis-leading, and unnecessarily restrictive.

As part of my study, I collected swatches of many factory-woven fabrics because I learned long ago that the textile industry knows what it's doing before it produces hundreds of yards of cloth. Photographs of many of those samples are included in this book. Studying commercial cloth can be beneficial to handweavers, and it has shown me some of the fallacies of following strict rules too closely, as well as providing a wealth of inspiration for my own experiments. While some factory fabric is not practical to reproduce on most handlooms, handweavers can achieve the effect of very sheer fabric, for example, using wider setts and heavier threads. It's also nice to know that some things that aren't practical on factory looms can be woven effectively on handlooms.

Choosing Colors

Woven fabric is three-dimensional, not two-dimensional, and we see iridescence because of the reflection of light from the ridges and valleys formed by the intersection of threads. Crumpling a fabric lets you see different angles at the same time, and deliberate texturing (pleats, puckers, gathers, smocking, and embossing) can accentuate color differences. Another important aspect of iridescent textiles is that there must be some visual contrast. A contrast in hues is desirable so that the color changes are more obvious at different angles. Sometimes, value contrast will keep the colors distinct.

Iridescence varies from dramatic to very subtle. You can create a fabric that will turn heads immediately or show nuances of color only apparent at second glance. There are many factors that influence the results, and they are often interdependent. Your choice of colors, yarns, and structure are very important.

Here are some of the common beliefs about weaving iridescent fabrics. I don't call them *myths* because you can produce iridescence using any of these criteria. However,

while there is some truth to all of them and a lot of truth to some of them, there is relatively little truth to some, and there are exceptions to every one.

You must use complements.
You must use saturated colors.
You must use colors of the same value.
You must cross solid colors.
You must use lustrous yarns.
You must use silk.
You must use fine thread.
You must use plain weave.
You must have a balanced weave.

Don't feel restricted by these "rules." It's a mistake to feel that you *must* follow a particular guideline. There are many ways to create exciting iridescent fabrics, and no doubt there are new options yet to be discovered!

Complementary Colors

The idea that you have to use complements is one of the most common beliefs about iridescent fabrics, and one I

The color contrast in these commercial swatches crossing complements produces good iridescence.

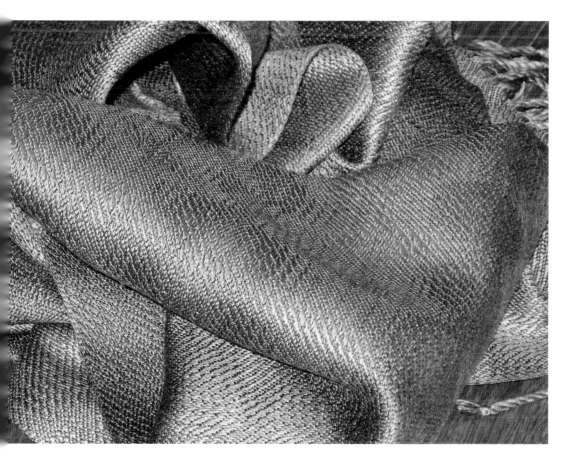

This scarf by Agnes Hauptli is dramatic with split complements of blue-green and orange. 16 shafts; parallel threadings in blue and green (echo). The warp is 30/2 silk, with a finer orange weft. Photo courtesy of Agnes Hauptli.

especially like to violate. It is true that crossing complements will virtually always produce iridescence, if other factors including weave structure are favorable. Complementary hues are as different as possible, and they provide a striking contrast that makes the colors distinct in the fabric.

Such contrast does not always produce the most pleasing results, although that's a matter of personal opinion. Just because a fabric is iridescent doesn't mean you'll like it! I find the combination of saturated red and green, for example, to be too jarring to suit my taste. Complements often produce disturbing visual vibrations, the effect I noticed in my first color sampler many years ago. However, I am grateful I chose red-violet and yellow-green for

||||||||||||||||||||||||||||||||||||||||||||||||||||||||||||||

Complements provide color contrast that can be beneficial when you want dramatic iridescence, particularly when using relatively heavy yarns or yarns without a lot of luster. When you work with colors that have strong contrast in value, distinct differences in hue can help.

my napkin sample because this combination produces dramatic iridescence that caught my attention . . . even though I didn't realize at the time that I was (or "should be") using complementary colors.

Mixing complements in paints produces dulled colors, browns and grays, and the same effect can happen in fabric when complementary colors show in equal amounts, especially if their values are similar. From increasing distances, these fabrics look more muddy than they do close-up. Crossing complementary colors can also dull the brilliance of individual components.

Split Complements, Triads, and Tetrads

If we could only achieve iridescence with complements, we might get bored quickly. Fortunately, each color on the color wheel has two split complements, and you can achieve good iridescence with either of them, giving you more options. There is still strong contrast between the colors, and sometimes the results might be more pleasing to you.

I used split complements of turquoise (blue-green) and red for many of my early samples because I knew they would produce good iridescence. I wanted to study many other factors besides color, including fiber, luster, value, thread size, beat, sett, and weave structure. Keeping

Split complements produce strong color contrast for good results.

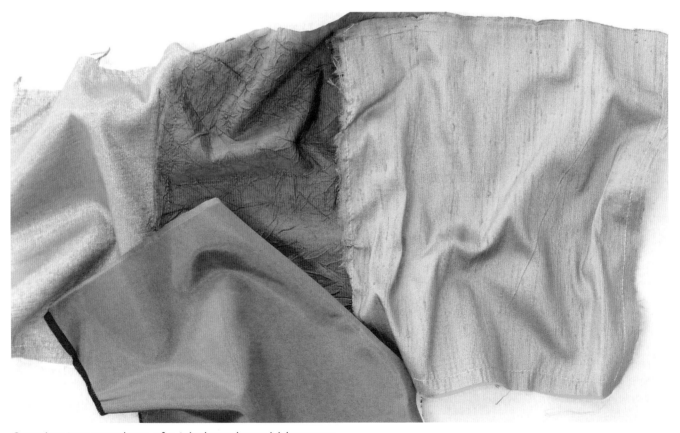

Crossing two members of a triad produces iridescence.

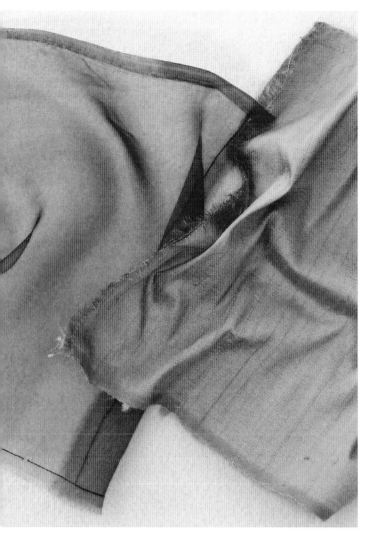

These iridescent factory-woven fabrics each include two components of tetrads.

the colors constant helped me analyze the results without being influenced by the color choice.

Choosing three colors equally spaced on the wheel means that they are more closely related than complements or split complements, but they are still distinct enough to tell apart easily. Crossing two components of a triad will usually produce good iridescence and will often be pleasing to the eye.

A square tetrad is composed of four colors equally spaced on the wheel, consisting of two pairs of complements. The pairs of the square that are not complements (in adjacent corners of the square) are different enough to give good iridescence in any combination. A rectangular tetrad has two pairs of complements, two pairs that are analogous, and two pairs that are parts of triads.

For either type of tetrad, the complements will work, and choosing two of the colors that are not complements will give you interesting options, usually with enough color contrast to produce good iridescence. Along with yellow-green and magenta, the additional two colors I chose for my napkin sampling and project were also complements, blue-green and red-orange. The four form a rectangular tetrad, although I wasn't aware of it at the time; in fact, I didn't realize I was using complementary colors.

I found more examples of commercial cloth in each category of split complements, triads, and tetrads than I did of the complementary combinations.

Analogous Colors

One of the most beautiful fabrics I ever saw was an antique Indian sari someone brought to one of my classes. This

Analogous combinations that include red-violet are:

Left: blue-violet, violet, red-violet (mostly cool)

Center: violet, red-violet, red (cool to warm)

Right: red-violet, red, red-orange (mostly warm)

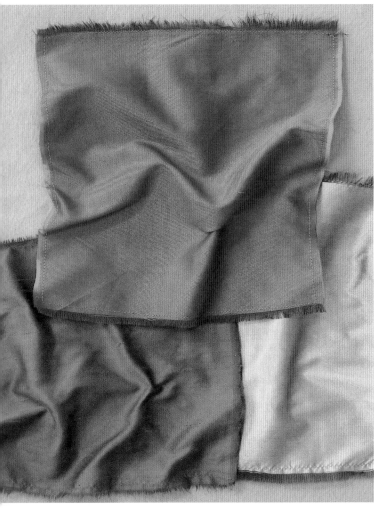

These three Asian silk fabrics are markedly iridescent despite the closely related colors in each. Even turquoise crossed with blue is effective here.

||||||||||||||||||||||||||||||||||||||||||||||||||||||||||||||||||

Virtually any color combination can be iridescent, as long as there is enough difference between the colors to tell them apart in the fabric, and other factors such as value and weave structure are favorable.

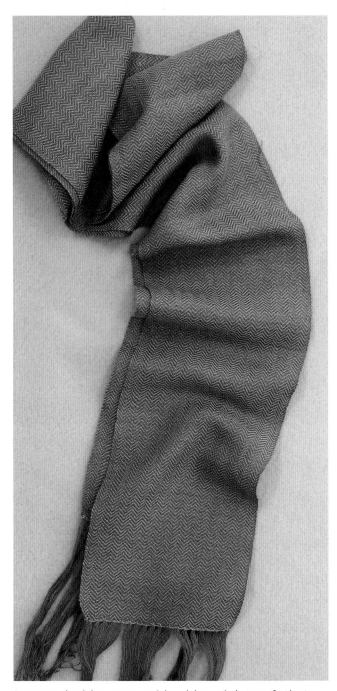

I crossed a blue warp with a blue-violet weft that was predominantly blue and of a lighter value. The colors are too similar to give good iridescence.

silk fabric was blue crossed with green and embroidered with real gold thread. There was nothing subtle about the iridescence, which was enhanced by the lustrous threads.

Since I wear only cool colors, I am particularly delighted to be able to achieve iridescence with the colors I most love. If your color palette is warmer, you can do the same. Analogous colors can be all warm or all cool or can include the transitional hues of red-violet or yellow-green.

As long as the colors you choose are distinct enough to tell apart in the fabric, they can be closely related. Some colors within the same hue family or even in adjacent hue families can be too similar to be effective in some cases.

A blue-green that is almost green (such as teal green) may not work well with a cool green but has possibilities with a warmer green. Blue-green that favors the blue component (such as turquoise) may work very well with

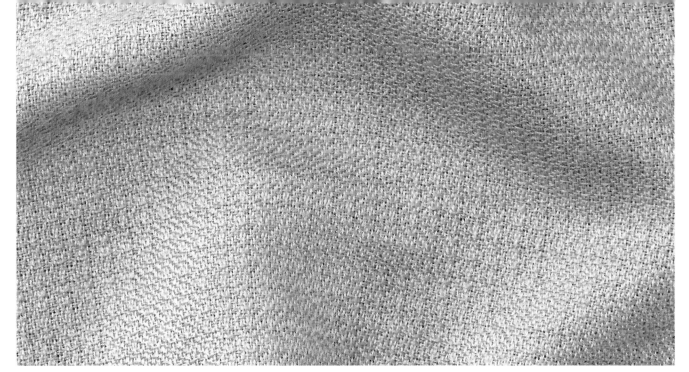

This pink and light blue blouse fabric, handwoven in 20/2 mercerized cotton, is opalescent. The choice of triadic colors provides effective color contrast, and the values are the same.

the same cool green, and even turquoise with a teal green within the same hue family may be distinct enough to be effective.

Color Saturation

It makes sense that an effect that depends on color will be more obvious the more color you have to work with. Brilliant colors produce brilliant results. It is more challenging to work with pastels, tints of brighter colors, but it's possible to produce beautiful iridescent fabric with light colors, especially if they are of the same value.

It's quite difficult, but not impossible, to achieve iridescence when one component is white because white is the maximum value and dilutes everything you cross it with. Even a small amount of white can overpower other colors.

Black, on the other hand, is commonly used with bright colors, since it makes all colors look more colorful. When crossed with a colored thread, black also adds a depth or shadow to the fabric that makes it more interesting as well as iridescent.

Saturated yellow, which has the lightest value of the natural spectrum, tends to dominate in a fabric, just as white does. A tint of yellow can be easier to work with unless there is strong color contrast.

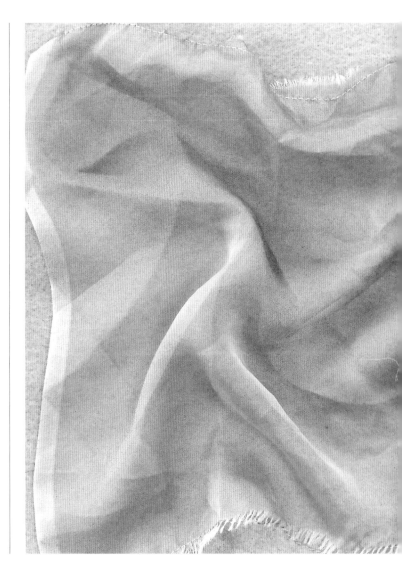

Here's a sheer commercial fabric, orange crossed with white, which shows good iridescence in both colors.

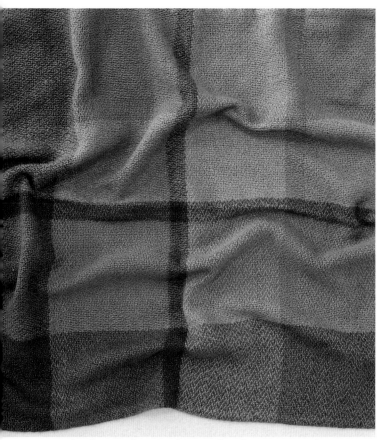

The four colors in this napkin form a tetrad, two pairs of complements, and they are not all the same value, although all the combinations are iridescent.

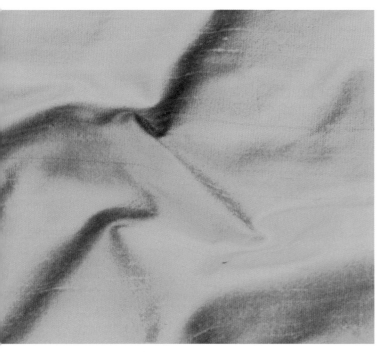

This Thai silk fabric, blue crossed with blue-green, is beautifully iridescent because of the lustrous yarn, balanced weave, and the use of colors of the same value.

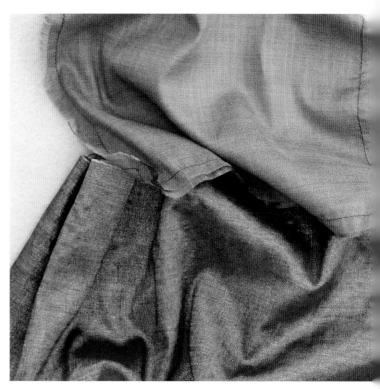

These factory-woven swatches show effective iridescence with complementary colors, despite considerable value contrast.

Value

When I discovered iridescence in my original napkin sample, I remembered having heard that you needed to use colors of the same value, and so I arbitrarily chose two additional colors off my shelf that I thought were of the same value as the red-violet and yellow-green I'd been using. They weren't. In fact, the original two colors were also not of the same value.

Value is one of the most important considerations when designing iridescent fabrics, and when things don't turn out the way you expect, too much value contrast may be the reason. Nevertheless, there are many good iridescent fabrics that do not use colors of the same value, and in some fabrics, a deliberate value contrast helps. It's even possible, although challenging, to make iridescent fabrics using only black and white.

If working with similar values was required, we would not be able to achieve iridescence with saturated violet (the darkest hue in the spectrum) crossed with saturated yellow (the lightest). These colors are complements, and they do give good iridescence; the color contrast overrides the value contrast in this case. Crossing blue and orange or some other complements gives similar results. You can also create good iridescence with distinct colors

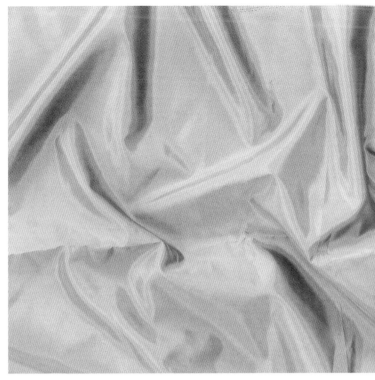

Crossing light colors or dark colors works best when values are similar. Choose colors of similar value when crossing two analogous colors, especially if the colors are very closely related. Value contrast is less of a hindrance when the colors are more distinct. When weaving fabric containing blocks of multiple colors, some difference in value seems more important, as it does with multiple colors at each point of interlacement. The value contrast helps you distinguish the colors.

of the same value. Saturated red and its complement, saturated green, have the same value. The more closely related the colors, the more important it seems to be to use similar values.

I've encountered difficulty working with a dark shade of green, often called hunter green, more than with any other color. For a while, I thought there might be something about that particular color that was different, but I've come to the conclusion that value contrasts are the reason for disappointing results.

This commercial swatch, dark green crossed with yellow, is not iridescent, even though the structure appears to be plain weave rather than satin. Iridescence was evidently not the intent of the designer, who used the dark green to give a rich bronze look to the cloth, much more interesting than if it were solid yellow.

This clasped-weft scarf with a dark green warp is not iridescent. There is apparently too much value contrast with the lighter wefts, which are analogous with the warp.

Crossing dark green with colors of the same or similar value produces good iridescence. As value contrast increases, the iridescence decreases.

Crossing Solid Colors

I used to think it was necessary not only to cross solid colors but also to have relatively large areas of crossed colors in order to see iridescence well. I changed my mind after looking carefully at a scarf I'd been given. This scarf has a solid yellow warp and a space-dyed weft with frequent color changes, so there are no significant areas where the same two colors cross. Yet it is iridescent. The weft colors are within a limited range—red-orange, red, and violet—and these colors would normally be iridescent with yellow.

I then wondered if it was possible to cross two different space-dyed yarns and achieve iridescence. I chose yarns with frequent color changes, each within a limited range of analogous colors: one in blue and blue-green and the other violet to red. Individually, these colors will produce iridescence with each other, and the same is true of the variegated yarns. One color family will work well when crossed with another color family as long as the colors are distinct enough to tell apart easily and the same colors are not included in both warp and weft.

The colors in the space-dyed weft interact effectively with the solid warp color. Scarf courtesy of the Arizona Federation of Weavers and Spinners Guilds, Fibers Through Time conference.

Although there are no significant solid areas of color crossing each other, the space-dyed yarns in warp and weft produce good iridescence throughout this scarf. 20/2 Tencel, yarn courtesy of Just Our Yarn.

Solid yarns in mixed colors, using constant color changes without obvious stripes, may have the same effect as a variegated yarn for producing iridescence when crossed with a solid color. This is easier to accomplish in the warp than in the weft, although you could use a space-dyed yarn as weft with a multicolored warp for a

|||||||||||||||||||||||||||||||||||||||||||||||||||||||||||||

Space-dyed yarn with analogous colors can create iridescence when crossed with contrasting solid colors or a space-dyed yarn with different analogous colors. Avoid a space-dyed yarn with many unrelated colors, which may not give effective results. Relatively short color segments are most effective, especially when weaving narrow projects.

similar result. Again, colors should be related in the warp and in the weft, but in different color families. This can be a useful way to use up small amounts of yarn.

Luster

Anything that enhances light reflection from an iridescent fabric will tend to make its color changes more noticeable, so a shiny yarn is always a good choice. Silk, rayon (including Tencel and bamboo), nylon, mercerized cotton, and some linens have an attractive sheen that produces pleasing results. Metallic yarns can also be effective if they do not overpower other yarn colors; not all fabrics with metallics are iridescent, however.

Like the other "rules," this one has exceptions. Dull yarns can also make iridescent fabrics, especially if the colors are quite different, or analogous colors have the same value.

Many iridescent Thai fabrics have a dull black warp and a lustrous silk weft. Although the luster contrast is

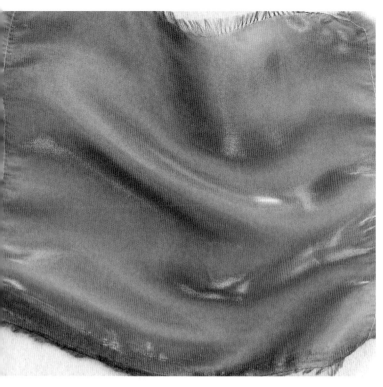

A brilliantly lustrous synthetic yarn makes this factory-woven fabric glow with iridescence.

IIIIIIIIIIIIIIIIIIIIIIIIIIIIIIIIIIIIIIIIIIIIIIIIIIIIIIIIIIIIIIIIIIIIIIIIII

A shiny yarn reflects light better than a dull one and enhances iridescence. If using yarns without luster, choose colors that are very distinct, or make sure they have the same value. If working with coarse yarns, luster is recommended to improve the iridescence. A very fine yarn that is not dominant in a fabric will show better if it has high luster, especially in contrast with a less lustrous yarn.

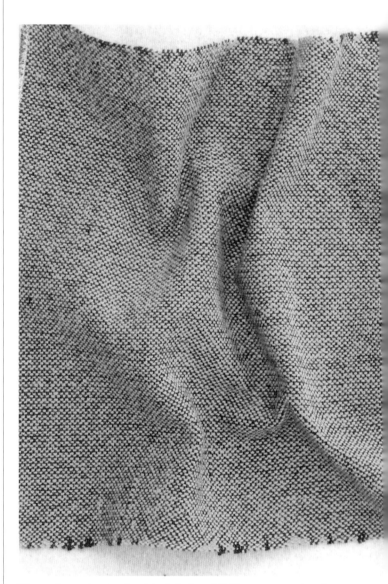

This coarse fabric, woven with heavy rayon, is very iridescent because of the high luster of the yarn and the distinct colors. Because the thread intersections are relatively large, you can always see both colors, while each color dominates at different angles.

There is no luster in this fabric of 8/2 unmercerized cotton, but it is still iridescent because I used split complementary colors that are quite distinct (turquoise warp and red weft).

Most wool yarns have little luster. This wool fabric is nonetheless iridescent because of the choice of dissimilar colors.

still effective, it probably is not deliberate. Thai weavers typically work on a very long warp, and black works well crossed with any other color. The warp yarn may be a less expensive yarn that is not silk. Deliberately choosing a matte yarn that is considerably lighter in value than a lustrous yarn used in the same fabric might tend to dampen some of the effect of the lighter yarn and help balance the iridescence.

Fiber Choice

Silk is a wonderful choice for iridescence because of its luster, and fortunately for our budgets, we have many other fiber choices as well. My collection of factory-woven fabrics proved to me that a wide range of fibers, including many synthetics, can produce wonderful iridescence.

IIIIIIIIIIIIIIIIIIIIIIIIIIIIIIIIIIIIIIIIIIIIIIIIIIIIIIIIIIIIIIII

Use silk if you have it, can afford it, and it suits your purpose, but don't feel restricted to using silk. There are many other excellent choices.

The idea that silk is required may have developed because so many iridescent Asian fabrics are silk. The less expensive silk yarns don't always have a lot of luster, and most rayons are more lustrous than the commonly available silks.

Thread Size

Not only are you supposed to use silk for iridescence, it must be gossamer silk, according to some rule makers. Fine silk is a delight, and my experiments have led me to work with finer yarns than I ever had before. However, not all weavers want to work at setts of 60 ends per inch (e.p.i.) or closer.

There is some truth to the idea that fine threads improve iridescence because in fine fabric, we no longer notice the individual thread intersections. The color change is more striking because each color reflects light as a uniform sheen uninterrupted by dots of another color. The coarser the yarns you work with, the more important other factors such as value and color choice tend to be.

You don't always have to use warp and weft yarns of the same weight. In some cases, particularly weaves such as sateen, turned taqueté, networked twills, and

Compare these swatches woven in plain weave with mercerized (pearl) cotton. All three are very iridescent because of the split complementary colors and the lustrous yarn. The swatch on the left is woven with 5/2 cotton, and no matter the orientation, you always see both colors, even though one will be dominant at a particular angle. The thread intersections are less obvious in the center swatch, in 10/2 cotton. The swatch on the right is woven with 20/2 cotton, and our eyes no longer notice the thread intersections.

Both of these scarves, woven on the same warp with the same yarns (space-dyed 20/2 Tencel), are iridescent because of the color choices. The plain-weave scarf on the bottom looks duller than the crêpe-weave scarf on the top. Yarn courtesy of Just Our Yarn.

self-pleating fabrics, a finer weft is often recommended and can still be effective. It can be helpful to use a lustrous yarn for the finer component in such a cloth.

What about Plain Weave?

The idea that you must use plain weave to achieve iridescence might have developed because most of the Asian silks are woven in plain weave. The long-standing traditions of producing iridescent fabrics in India, Thailand, and neighboring countries make these the standard in many people's minds. Fine plain-weave cloth might seem more magical because of its very simplicity. Also, plain weave is quite often a balanced weave, displaying crossed threads in equal quantities, so each color gets equal billing.

In fact, plain weave is almost never the best choice for iridescence. Weave structures with floats, distinct twill lines, and patterns that create uniform planes reflect light better and create more dramatic results.

Plain weave is actually the most difficult structure for weaving perfect fabric. Any inconsistencies in beat, denting, tension, and selvedge turns will be evident when crossing different colors, and the results can be humbling even for experienced weavers!

Balanced Weaves

It makes sense that a balanced weave will give crossed colors equal opportunity to show, so it is often a good goal to strive for in plain weave and many twills. A balanced weave is usually defined as having the same size and spacing of warp and weft; balanced twills are distinguished by a twill diagonal of 45 degrees. Fortunately, because few weavers create perfect fabrics, perfect balance is not required for iridescence. A ratio of one-third of one color to two-thirds of another can still be iridescent if there is enough color or value contrast. Using an unbalanced weave may help keep a high-value yarn from overpowering a darker color.

There are many weave structures that do not produce a balanced fabric and yet can be very iridescent, including some that under normal circumstances are quite weft- or warp-dominant. Other factors such as color contrast, luster, texture, twist and twill direction, and a contrast in thread size can produce surprising results in fabrics that might not be expected to be iridescent.

Additional Color
Considerations

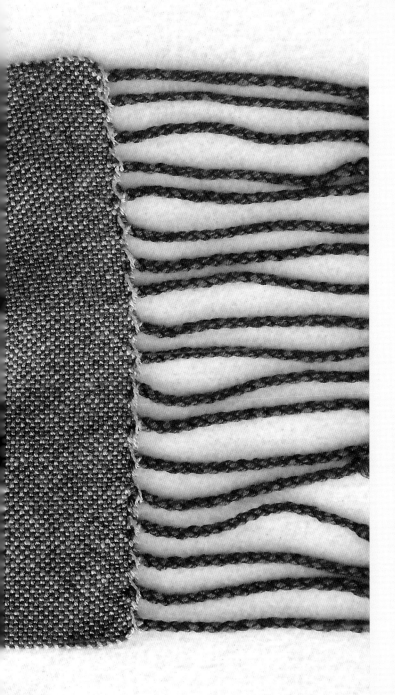

CHAPTER FOUR

Dealing with High-Contrast Values

Yellow, white, and tints of other colors can be difficult to work with because of their high values, especially when crossed with darker colors. When blending paints, for example mixing blue with yellow to get green, artists use a much smaller proportion of the lighter color. In weaving, it's harder to keep the lighter color from dominating just by using fewer threads of it.

One approach would be to use a tint of the darker color instead of a saturated hue, making the values more similar. Choosing a strong color contrast (such as the complements violet and yellow) can also be effective.

Another option is to use yarns of different sizes. A very fine thread of a lighter color crossed with a darker, heavier yarn can give the darker yarn more prominence in the mix.

Some weave structures and layered fabrics may help subdue a lighter color. An unbalanced twill can sometimes be iridescent and might be effective with the darker color dominant (3/1 twill with the darker color in the warp, for example). Other strongly warp-dominant or weft-dominant weaves and pleated fabrics are worth trying. Use of luster contrast may also work, such as combining a very shiny yarn of the dark color with a low-luster yarn of the higher value.

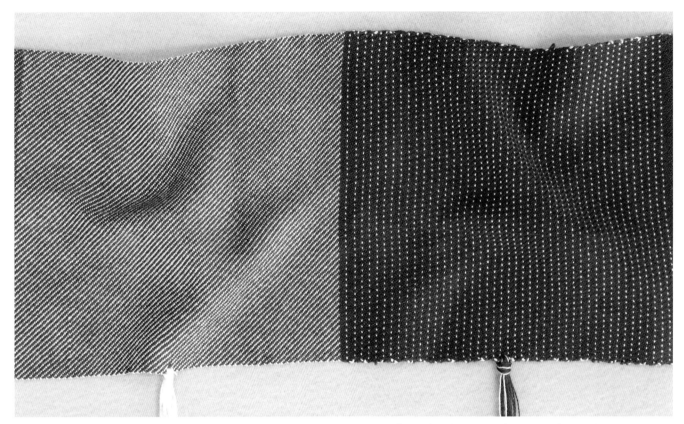

In the sample on the left, yellow overpowers the dark green in 2/2 twill, although there is a hint of iridescence. The swatch on the right, with a dark green yarn used both in warp and weft, has occasional picks of yellow. The yellow (the same size yarn) is still prominent, and the dotted fabric is not iridescent.

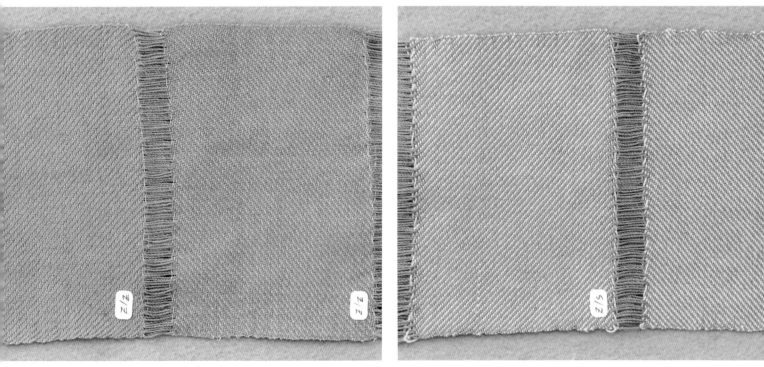

These samples (left) cross a tint of violet with a much finer yellow sewing thread, producing iridescence without having the yellow overwhelm the purple. The warp is 10/2 mercerized cotton at a normal twill sett, and the weft is beaten lightly to maintain a 45-degree twill angle. Using the same size thread for the yellow weft (right) makes the yellow more dominant.

This plain-weave swatch has a 20/2 cotton warp with a denser-than-usual sett, crossed by a lustrous, finer weft of high value.

The close-up view of this pleated shawl by Wendy Morris shows that the fabric is predominantly blue and green, with just a few threads of orange at the center of the pleats. The full view shows how effective this is in balancing the colors for a dramatic iridescent effect. 12 shafts; 60/2 silk. Photo courtesy of Wendy Morris.

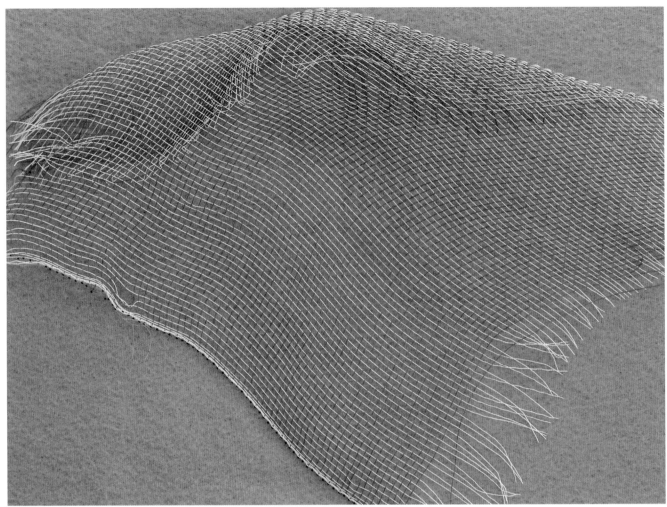

This fabric of monofilament nylon ("floral wrap") in an open plain weave is iridescent in purple and white.

Some colorways of monofilament nylon *floral wrap* (see page 78) cross a color with white, yet are surprisingly iridescent. The unusual effectiveness of these white/color mixes may be partly the result of the very open plain-weave structure, with white threads separated by enough distance that they don't overpower the color. This also works in some fine, sheer fabrics.

The Ultimate Value Contrast

Can a black-and-white fabric be iridescent? It sounds oxymoronic to produce iridescence without actually using color, and while it's one of the biggest challenges because of the extreme value contrast, it is possible. Most fabrics that cross black and white blend to gray, and any iridescence is subdued. However, some unusual fabrics in strongly warp-dominant and weft-dominant structures exhibit the phenomenon.

The best black-and-white iridescent fabrics I've seen and woven have been satins/sateens and striped and pleated fabrics, which might seem improbable and are certainly nontraditional. In the case of satin (easier to weave as turned satin or sateen), a distinct thread-size contrast allows the heavier black tie-down threads to spread apart the finer white threads just enough to show through.

Color Mixing

Artists blend paints to create different colors, a nonreversible process. As mentioned earlier, mixing complementary paint colors creates browns and grays. In weaving, we can sometimes achieve optical color mixing by crossing certain colors, while maintaining their ability to produce iridescence. A "third" color of gray or brown is particularly noticeable when crossing complements or secondary or tertiary colors that show the influence of their component hues. The actual colors of the threads are distinguishable at the same time.

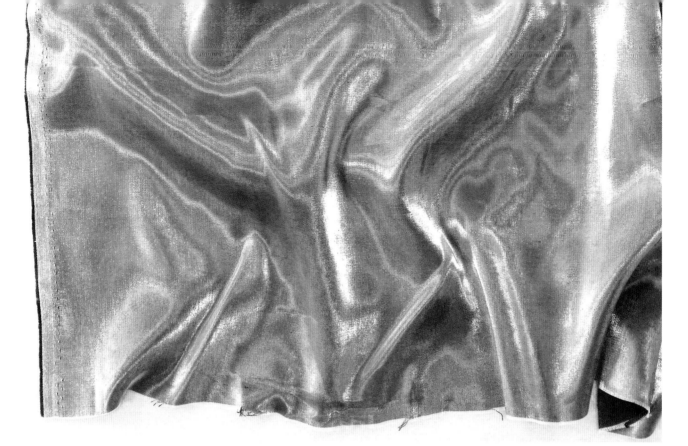

This factory-woven satin, with a fine, lustrous white thread and a heavier black background, is one of the best examples of black-and-white iridescence I've seen.

This handwoven sateen is also effective. I used 20/2 pearl cotton for the black warp at 80 e.p.i. (ends per inch) and a very fine lustrous sewing thread for the white weft, with 32 picks per inch. This is a 7-end, 8-shaft turned satin.

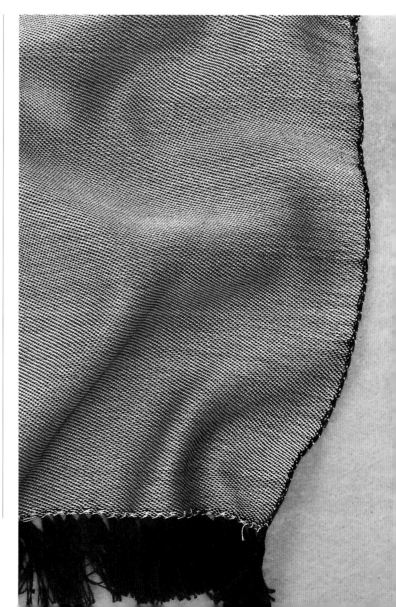

With colors that are not primaries, I most often see the blended effect with blue-violet and yellow-green (part of a triad) when they cross each other. Viewed from a moderate distance at a low angle, this combination appears to go gray, while you can still see the individual components and achieve iridescence with them. This particular blended effect may be because of what some artists refer to as "hidden complements" (David E. Cuin, *Take Control of Color: Creating Drama and Impact in Arts and Crafts*; see Recommended Resources, p. 132). The violet in blue-violet is the complement of the yellow in yellow-green, the green is a mix of yellow and blue, and color mixing can occur, especially when the yarn colors are of similar value. We can normally achieve gray by weaving with gray threads or by crossing white and black threads. While painters sometimes avoid them, I like these "sophisticated" grays and browns created without using neutral colors.

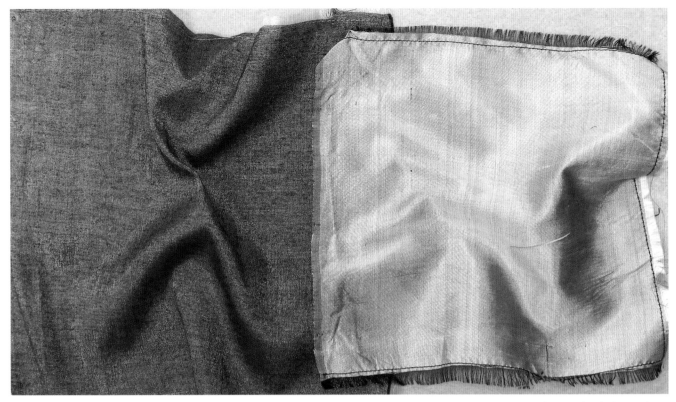

These swatches of black crossed with white look gray. Color shifting is subtle in the sample on the left, and a little better in the swatch on the right.

The apparent gray in this cross of blue-violet and dark yellow-green (left) is an example of optical color mixing. At the same time, the component colors produce iridescence. On the right, crossing complements (here, dark red-violet and dark yellow-green) tends to dull both colors and produce a brownish mix.

This striped fabric alternating warp- and weft-dominant twills is iridescent because of its pleats. The shift of colors at the center of the sample is the result of changing the treadling: Warp-faced twill ridges can become weft-faced valleys, and vice versa. Just as it is the three-dimensional texture of cloth that makes us see iridescence, pleats act as exaggerated ridges, which reflect light, and the black and white appear to ripple across the fabric as it moves.

This factory-woven fabric from a taffeta (plain weave) skirt crosses a brilliant red-violet (fuchsia) with bright yellow. It also appears to contain orange, because of optical mixing. The orange effect is intentional, evidenced by the solid orange fabric used to line the skirt.

Crossing some colors that are not complements produces brighter color blending. Yellow crossed with red can give the effect of a third color, orange. Yellow crossed with blue can look green, especially if the values are not too different. Blue crossed with red or red-violet gives the effect of purple. These blends are especially evident at a distance. Color blends can sometimes interfere with iridescence, especially when working with analogous colors.

Optical color mixing is most effective in plain weave, where the close interlacement and lack of floats can be compared to Pointillist paintings that use dots of color to give the effect of certain hues. This is one instance where plain weave can be a better choice than a weave with floats.

Even in heavier 10/2 cotton, crossing fuchsia with yellow adds orange to the mix in this handwoven sample. This is more evident in the plain-weave fabric on the left than in the 2/2 twill on the right, where the reflection from the prominent twill line of the high-value yellow subdues the darker pink.

IIIIIIIIIIIIIIIIIIIIIIIIIIIIIIIIIIIIIIIIIIIIIIIIIIIIIIIIIIIIIIII

When attempting color mixing, choose plain weave for the best results. Yarns of similar values are often the best choices, although some value contrast can work in some cases. Sample color combinations in various configurations to help plan pleasing results, especially before working with finer threads that will require more preparation and weaving time.

Working with Multiple Colors

Luxury silk fabrics have been woven in Lyon, France, since the 15th century. Well over a hundred years ago, handweavers in Lyon were weaving fine silk fabric called chameleon taffeta. Iridescent in three colors, all three colors were present at every thread intersection. This production continued until 1950. An attempt to revive the industry very early in the 21st century may have been unsuccessful, given that Internet sites describing the process and the Chameleon Workshop revival disappeared quickly. (Current websites about chameleon silk and the Chameleon Workshop refer to quite different products and studios.)

If you alternate colors in warp or weft in a normal fashion, you obtain striped fabrics that may show a hint of iridescence, but it is disappointing. As adjacent warp threads rise and fall, or weft colors alternate in successive picks, they are alternately crossed by different sets of threads, and this interferes with a uniform reflection of light.

French three-color silks were woven with a single warp color and two weft colors in the same pick, which were not allowed to cross each other. The weft color order was maintained from one pick to the next, so that viewed from one end of the fabric, a single weft color appeared, and from the other end, the other weft color was dominant. The warp, of a different color than the wefts, added the third color to the fabric. Woven by hand in fine silk and plain weave, these were magical fabrics!

The French weavers devised a complex shuttle to hold two threads, to keep them from crossing and to keep the same color order for successive picks. For most handweavers, weaving with a single warp color and two weft colors is easiest with two shuttles and is no more difficult than any other 2-shuttle weave. Don't try to wind

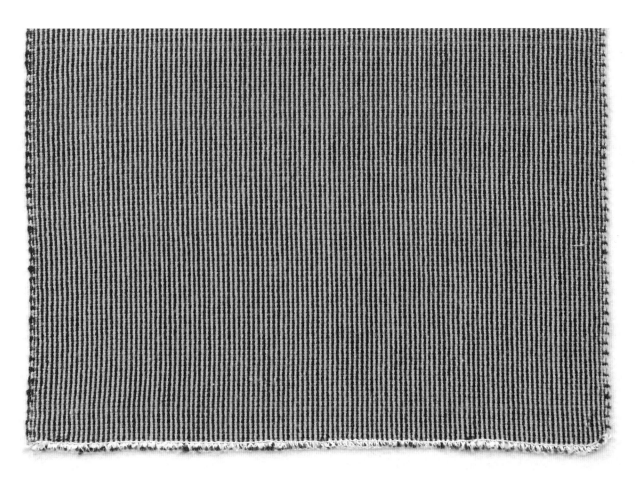

Fabric threaded with colors that alternate on different shafts does not display good iridescence. This sample alternates turquoise and red in both warp and weft and shows warpwise stripes on one face, weftwise stripes on the other.

the two wefts on the same bobbin or pirn; the threads will cross in the shed and interfere with the iridescence.

Using a double-bobbin shuttle does not work well. The wefts have more tendency to cross, especially where they enter the shed, and it takes longer to align them than it would to use separate shuttles. Also, used normally, a double-bobbin shuttle reverses the color order with each pick, and it's important to keep the same wefts in the same order, which would require rotating the shuttle (bottom to top or top to bottom) for each row.

This unusual three-color Asian silk has one warp color (turquoise) and magenta and orange wefts that were probably wound together on the same shuttle. No attempt was made to keep the wefts separate, so they cross each other frequently. The fabric still has lovely iridescence because of the color choice, luster, and fine threads, but it is not as wondrous as it would be if the wefts were carefully aligned.

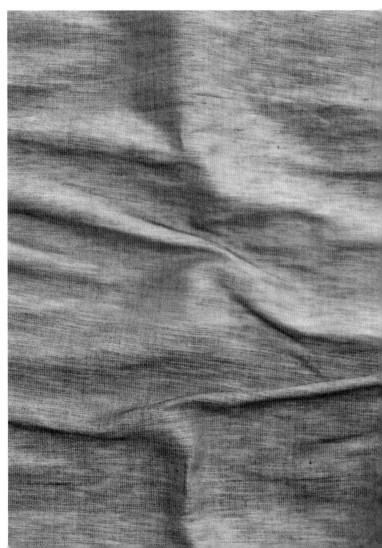

Throw the two shuttles from the same side, one color following the other in the same shed. To best prevent the wefts from crossing, throw the first shuttle, close the shed, beat, then reopen the same shed and throw the second shuttle. This is especially important in dry climates, with fine rayon and other "flyaway" threads. If the threads are less prone to static electricity, you can usually open the shed once, throw the two shuttles in succession, leaving the second weft at a slightly higher angle, close the shed, and beat after making sure the wefts don't cross, especially where they entered the shed. Beating on a closed shed keeps the wefts aligned. Experiment to see what works best for the yarns you're using. To maintain the consistent color effect, use the same order of weft colors for each pick.

Starting in 1890, attempts were made to create similar fabrics on automated looms in Lyon. Using two colors alternating in the warp and one color in the weft, the results were said to be inferior. I'm uncertain whether the warps were functioning separately or as a pair; if woven with very fine silk at more than 100 e.p.i., they most likely were sleyed in groups of multiple threads.

A handweaver's inclination, as it was for the industry, is to put two colors in the warp and weave with a single weft color and one shuttle. My first attempts, using paired warps in individual heddles on the same shaft but sleyed in the same reed dent, were unsuccessful. The finer the threads in this situation, the more they will cross each other, and the effect of uneven stripes was not what I wanted.

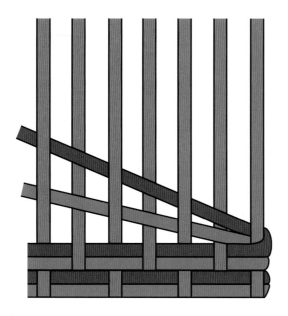

Working with two wefts in the same pick.

This fabric has paired warps on the same shafts in separate heddles and in the same dents of the reed. Some warps crossed each other, interrupting the reflection of light and putting the colors out of order.

I then reasoned that to prevent warps from crossing each other, they needed to be sleyed in separate dents. This will work with single sleying or with two warps per dent, but the adjacent threads on the same shaft cannot be in the same dent. This is most likely why the factory-loomed silks were not successful. At a sett of 120 e.p.i., for example, this would require single-sleying a 120-dent reed (extremely fragile and difficult to sley, if there is such a thing) or double-sleying a 60-dent reed—still a fragile and tricky piece of equipment to work with and not practical for factory looms.

Handweavers can successfully alternate two colors in the warp with coarser threads suitable for a twill sett of

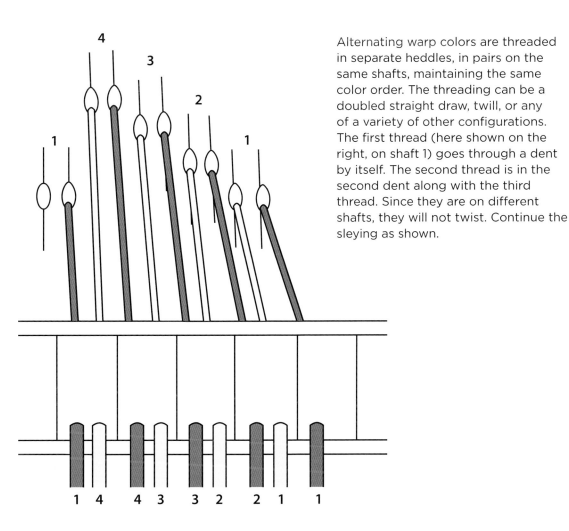

Alternating warp colors are threaded in separate heddles, in pairs on the same shafts, maintaining the same color order. The threading can be a doubled straight draw, twill, or any of a variety of other configurations. The first thread (here shown on the right, on shaft 1) goes through a dent by itself. The second thread is in the second dent along with the third thread. Since they are on different shafts, they will not twist. Continue the sleying as shown.

||||||||||||||||||||||||||||||||||||||||||||||||||||||||||||

When working with fine threads and a close sett, threading and sleying must be precise, or any inconsistency will show. For the same reason, warp tension must be uniform. Good vision and lighting are crucial. Sampling a few rows before you start the actual project will show any errors, and it's worth spending the time to correct them. It's not unusual for me to have to resley a fine doubled warp to correct errors.

30 to 60 e.p.i., double-sleyed in the reed using a normal threading hook. Any sley order other than single or double will not work; putting more than two colors in the warp functioning together would require single sleying. Closely dented reeds are available from some dealers, most often by special order. Depending on the reeds you have available and the yarn you intend to use, the sett may not be ideal, and you may have to adjust the beat accordingly.

Since we can weave with alternating warp colors, we can use two additional colors in the weft, following the same directions as for weaving with a single warp color, and achieve four-color iridescence. Every thread intersection contains all the colors.

A doubled warp and/or weft creates a basketweave or modified basketweave structure, with two-thread floats even when woven as plain weave. Choose a twill sett when using two colors in the warp, as close as your available reed will allow for the yarn you choose. I have used 60/2 silk, doubled, at 60 e.p.i. in a 30-dent reed, and a relatively gentle beat for a doubled-weft scarf. The normal plain-weave sett for this yarn would be 35 e.p.i.. For projects using 20/2 rayon or 20/2 cotton, I use a sett of 48 e.p.i. using a 24-dent reed; 8/2 Tencel works well at 30 e.p.i. for plain weave (sleyed double in a 15-dent reed) and requires a very light beat for 2/2 twill. The rayon sewing thread I used for the scarf at the top of page 44 would normally be sleyed closer than 60 e.p.i., but

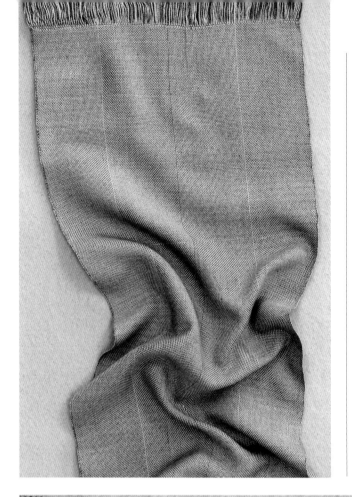

The silk in this four-color scarf is not as lustrous as rayon, but the effect is still beautiful, and the hand of the fabric is wonderful. Warp colors are red and yellow; wefts are blue and green. 60/2 silk sett at 60 e.p.i., basketweave. Yarn courtesy of RedFish DyeWorks.

In this detail of the silk scarf above, the apparent stripes in the warp (shown horizontally) are the result of changing the order of the warp colors every two inches. There is a similar effect with the two weft colors. These illusional stripes are only visible at certain angles.

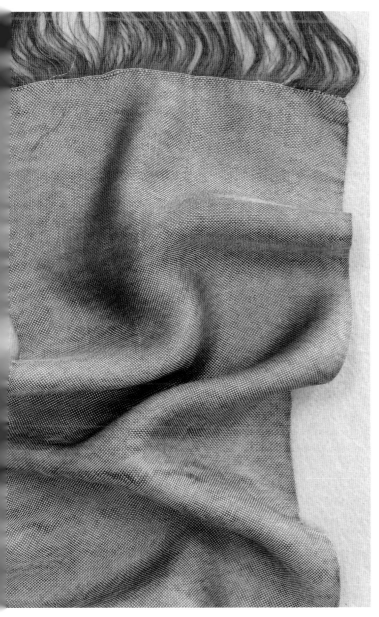

This four-color scarf has two warp and two weft colors at every point of interlacement. This plain-weave fabric was woven with rayon sewing thread at 60 e.p.i., which was the closest sett I could use with the 30-dent reed I had available. It required a very gentle beat. Sleying the slippery rayon was difficult because it tended to fall out of the reed unless taped down temporarily.

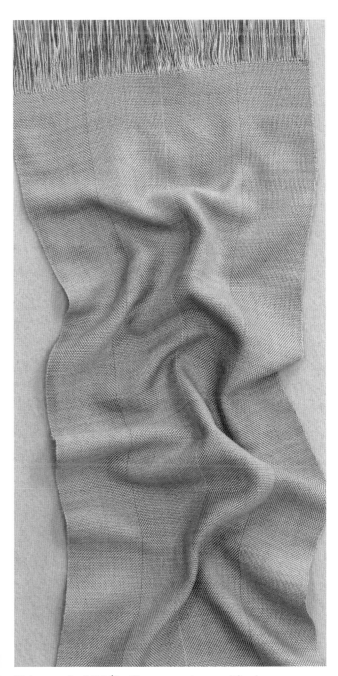

This scarf of 60/2 silk, woven in modified basketweave, has two warp colors, orange and yellow. There are three additional colors in the weft, blue-violet, red-violet, and blue-green. Yarn courtesy of RedFish Dyeworks.

my 30-dent reed was the finest I had available. Consequently, I had to beat the fabric very gently to maintain a balanced weave.

Unless you can single-sley a reed, you are limited to using two alternating colors in the warp. However, it's possible to weave five-color fabrics using three additional weft colors, all in the same pick. This requires three shuttles and a similar technique for aligning the wefts. Using more

than three wefts in a pick is not practical. Choosing compatible colors can be the most challenging part of these projects and benefits from sampling with coarser yarns.

In the three scarves shown on these two pages, I used a color-and-weave effect called "log cabin" to create apparent two-inch (5.1 cm) stripes in both warp and weft, so that all the colors would be more obvious no matter what the angle of view. This is a simple color alternation,

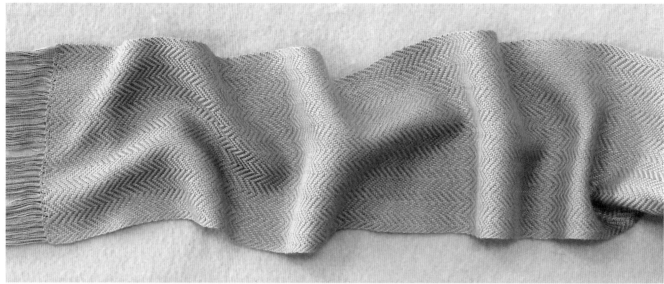

Woven on a point twill threading, this four-color scarf in 20/2 mercerized cotton has orange and pink in the warp and blue and green in the weft. The sett is 48 e.p.i., doubled in a 24-dent reed.

starting by alternating colors A and B in the same order for the desired width or length, then switching to B-A for the next section. The change in color order is more obvious in the silk scarves than in the rayon scarf. The "stripes" are illusional, and the effect is unattractive when the fabric is viewed flat, while quite striking when the scarves are "artfully crumpled."

You are not limited to plain weave when using the French technique and my variations. Most often a balanced weave will work best, so that both warp and weft

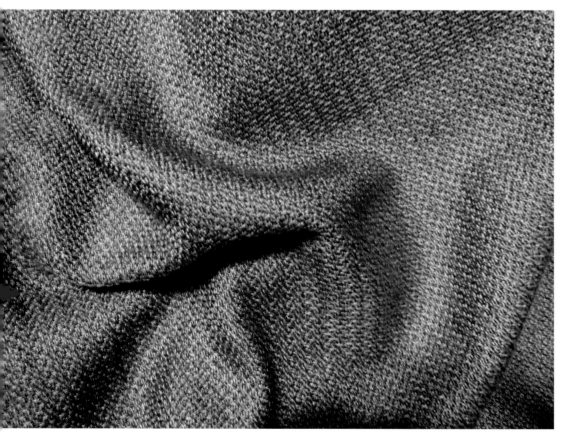

This four-color silk shawl uses the French method of aligning red and gold wefts in the same pick. Alternating blue and green warps are on different shafts and do not rise as a pair, yet still show a hint of iridescence. Twill, woven in 60/2 silk by Judy Hanninen, in association with the Allegheny River Textile ARTS Studio. Photo courtesy of Judy Hanninen.

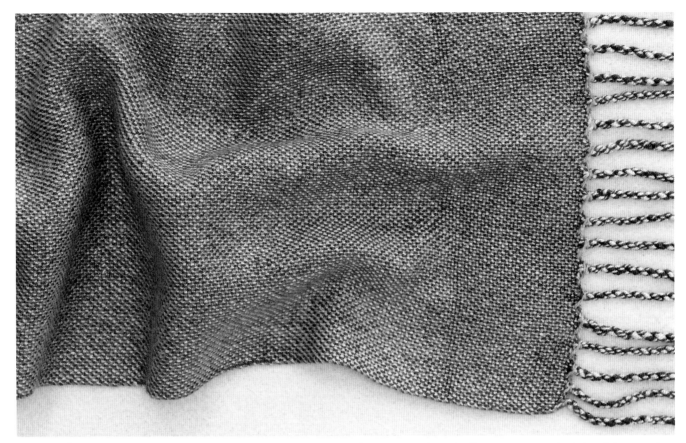

These 8/2 Tencel scarves are woven in plain weave with the same colors (yellow-green, red-violet, blue, and green) in different configurations. Although the iridescent effect is subtle because all colors are visible at any angle, the color interactions are interesting in this relatively heavy fabric.

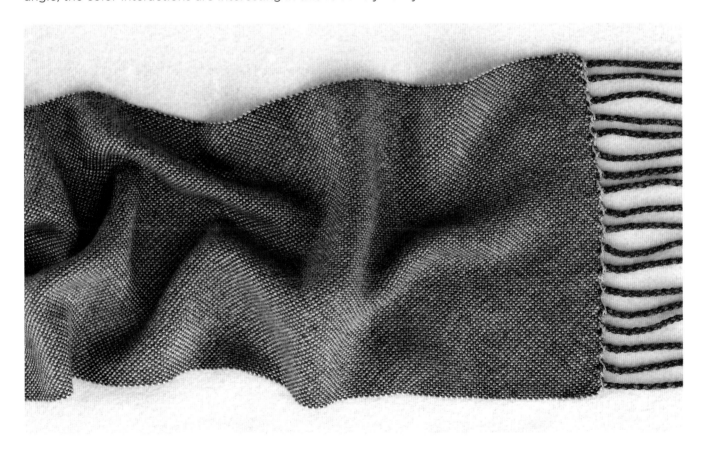

colors will be evident. Numerous twill-based weave structures, including some weft-dominant plaited twills, can be quite effective as long as they allow the perpendicular threads to show through.

A doubled straight-draw threading, 1-1-2-2-3-3-4-4, gives more treadling options than 1-1-3-3-2-2-4-4 (an alternate threading for basketweave). Different threadings such as point twill, with doubled warps, work well. Use as many shafts as you wish. The potential of using doubled warp and weft colors this way in complex weaves has yet to be explored extensively!

When you work with paired warps and/or wefts in this technique, the yarns must be easy to tell apart in order to show their colors from different angles. The distinction can be in hue, value, or both. Some value contrast does seem to help in this case. My preference is to use warm colors in one direction and cool colors in the other. However, some interesting combinations can result by combining cool and warm colors in either direction, and these may be less likely to appear as mixed colors and retain their individuality. With two colors in the warp or weft, it doesn't matter the order you thread and weave them, as long as you're consistent. When working with three colors in the warp and/or weft, it makes sense to separate analogous colors with a third unrelated color to keep the similar colors from blending.

With four colors, two each in the warp and weft, there are six possible color combinations (disregarding which color is on the left in the warp pairs or on the bottom of the weft pairs). The fabrics will look similar, but there will be slight differences, especially if the weave is not perfectly balanced. Sampling can show which combinations are most effective and suit your preference and is a good idea if closely related warps or wefts might tend to blend rather than remain distinct. Also, warps and wefts that are complements may cause a gray or brown effect that dampens the iridescence.

Heavier threads, such as 8/2 Tencel or 10/2 pearl cotton, are less effective for this multicolored effect since the thread intersections are more apparent. While fine threads are most suitable, coarser fabrics can still be attractive and look complex, even in plain weave.

It is possible to sley these yarns singly in a 30-dent reed, allowing for a three-color warp. Although weaving with more than three warp colors or weft colors using this technique is possible, it will compromise the stability and practicality of the cloth.

This Tencel scarf has three warp colors and three additional weft colors, woven in three-thread basket-weave at 30 e.p.i., and sleyed singly in a 30-dent reed. I used a plain-weave treadling rather than twill, which would have resulted in six-thread floats. The warp colors are turquoise, gold, and orange; the wefts are light magenta, dark blue-violet, and green. This 8/2 yarn is almost too heavy for the fine reed.

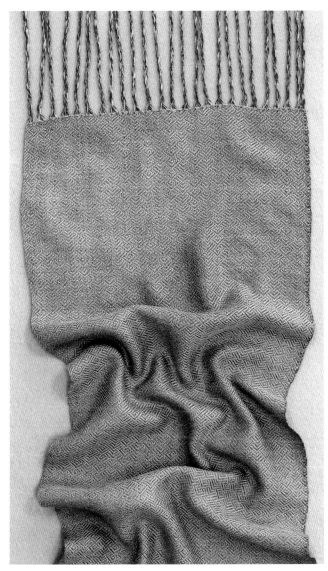

In this four-color scarf, the blue and green wefts tend to blend and look turquoise. Viewed from different angles, the wefts maintain their individual colors. 60/2 silk, 8-shaft plaited twill.

Other Multiple-Color Options

Another way of making a four-color fabric uses paired warp colors, as in the French method described above, and clasped-weft technique to add two weft colors. In this case, the entire fabric shows only three colors at any particular intersection, since the wefts are side by side in the same shed instead of being in contact selvedge to selvedge. Clasped weft adds interesting patterning and can be woven with as few as two shafts (doubled plain weave) or with more complex structures.

An exciting way of achieving iridescence in multiple colors is to use double weave with spaced warps and wefts. This is also a practical way of creating a sheer,

Inspired by Carry Wilcox, this four-color scarf in 8/2 Tencel has bonus patterning from clasped-weft technique and the crêpe weave treadling. See page 125 for instructions.

layered fabric without weaving with tiny threads. One of the projects in this book (Double-Weave Scarf, page 118) uses four colors in six different configurations on the same warp to show off the colors in various ways. Closely spaced warps at the selvedges space and stabilize the wefts in the open areas. I prefer to use two extra shafts to weave warp-dominant plain weave at the selvedges (requiring six shafts for the fabric), but 4-shaft weavers

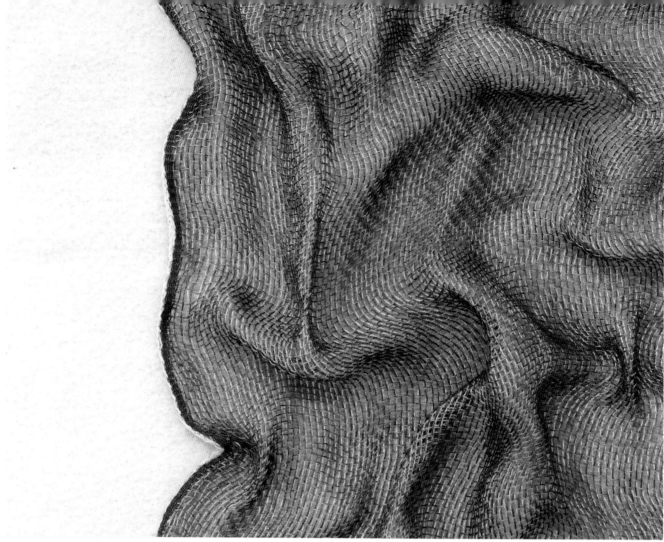

Inspired by Elaine Plaisance, this open-weave fabric allows the colors from the lower layer—especially the high-value yellow—to show through to the surface. Placing the yellow yarn on the bottom layer keeps it from being dominant over the surface colors.

can use closely spaced warps at the edges instead. The structures are slightly different; with six shafts, the selvedges are a single layer contrasted with tubular double weave in the open areas. With four shafts, the entire fabric has two layers connected at the sides. Although not suitable for all uses, this open-weave fabric is surprisingly stable and is appropriate for scarves. Most distortions in the double weave can be corrected easily by pulling gently on the bias.

Marian Stubenitsky, author of *Weaving with Echo and Iris*, has experimented with two and four warp colors in double weave, with two additional weft colors, using echo threadings. She recommends a value contrast in each layer to keep the colors distinct. She avoids crossing complements, because of the dulling effect, and advises against using analogous or monochromatic colors together in warp or weft. Marian recommends a strong color and value contrast in both warp and weft.

The same suggestions should also be appropriate in the multicolored fabrics pairing colors on the same shafts or in the same sheds, using the French technique.

Warp versus Weft—Does It Matter?

When I wove numerous samples in blue-green and red, I always kept the turquoise yarn in the warp. Afterward, I wondered if it would have made a difference if I'd chosen red for the warp instead, so I sampled to see what would happen. It did make a difference, even when I tried for a carefully balanced weave. A red warp was more dominant than a turquoise warp in identical structures and tended to overpower the blue. One reason might be that the finished sett in a fabric is often closer than in a weave designed to be balanced, because of draw-in. When a temple is not used, the effective sett in a fabric sleyed at 24 e.p.i., with 15 percent draw-in/shrinkage in width, may be closer to 28 e.p.i., so if the fabric is woven with 24 picks per inch (2.5 cm), it may end up slightly warp-dominant.

This inspired experiments to place blocks side by side, alternating warp and weft colors in the blocks: turquoise weft on red warp, red on turquoise. My theory was that at any angle, one block would show one dominant color and the adjacent block the other. My attempt with warp- and weft-dominant twills (3/1 and 1/3), probably the easiest way to approach the challenge, was unsuccessful, even though some other fabrics with unbalanced twills have worked satisfactorily.

Double-weave blocks do give the desired effect of shifting block colors, as long as you weave whichever warp color is on the top layer with the opposite weft color, and vice versa. (The popular 8-shaft pattern often called "windowpane checks" normally weaves solid blocks of color, weft A on warp A and weft B on warp B. My alternate version reverses the common weft color order.)

I wanted a scarf fabric with this effect that would drape nicely. Even in fine (20/2) pearl cotton, double weave forms too stiff a fabric, more appropriate for a vest or jacket than a scarf.

When the weave structure is unbalanced because of the float pattern, color orientation can be even more important. I wove fabric in a plaited twill with 20/2 rayon, with red and yellow in the warp and blue and green in the weft, using the French technique for multiple colors. The cooler weft colors showed well, and the warm warp colors blended to look like copper. Then I experimented with the same yarns, structure, sett, and treadling, using the cool colors in the warp and the warm ones in the weft. The red and yellow wefts overpowered the warp colors, and the overall effect was an orange fabric with little iridescence.

I find I like at least one secondary or tertiary color better in combinations, especially with primaries: for example, blue-green rather than blue with red or yellow. While these are personal preferences, the non-primary colors show the influence of their component hues, making the fabric more interesting.

Woven the usual way, this fabric alternates solid colors and is not iridescent (left). When woven with the opposite weft color (right), all blocks contain both colors, and the blocks appear to shift color as the angle of view changes.

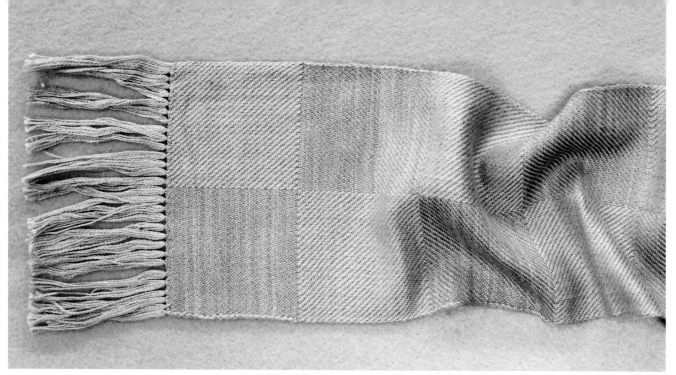

This 20/2 silk scarf, woven in unbalanced twill blocks, is not really iridescent, despite the use of complementary colors.

The overall color effect is strikingly different in these two fabrics, woven in the same 8-shaft plaited twill, with the same four colors. The only difference is in the orientation of the colors, warp versus weft. With the warm colors in the warp (left), the cooler weft colors show well. When the warm colors are in the weft (right), the cool warps hardly show at all, and iridescence is greatly reduced. Without needing to analyze the weave structure, these results suggest that these are weft-dominant fabrics.

This sampler in 10/2 cotton helped me choose pleasing color combinations for multicolored projects in finer yarns.

The more colors you put into a fabric, the more you risk ending up with "muddy" combinations. When making color choices, especially colors I haven't worked with very often, and especially when my finished project requires fine threads, I sample with heavier yarns (such as 10/2 pearl cotton) in similar colors to pick pleasing combinations, trying the desired colors in various configurations. Using a computer drafting program will give even quicker results, at least to weed out the more unpleasant combinations before you sample.

Choosing Yarns

Of the companies producing yarn, relatively few cater specifically to weavers, because the handweavers' market is much smaller than the knitters', for example. Consequently, the availability of weaving yarn changes as companies switch their focus or go out of business, and yarns and colors are frequently discontinued. Also, different yarns are available in different countries, where finding products comparable to some of those I mention in this book may be challenging.

Despite these challenges, weavers have a wealth of yarns to choose from in different fibers, sizes, and colors. Internet shopping makes it easy to compare products and prices (and has contributed to the disappearance of independent weaving stores, for which I encourage your support, although many of them now have websites).

As for any other aspect of weaving, choose yarns appropriate for the desired purpose. It should be possible for you to find yarn that will produce iridescence no matter what the intended use, as long as you keep in mind the many factors that influence the results: fiber content, size, twist, luster, color (including value, temperature, and saturation), and weave structure.

Beware of buying a yarn unseen, based merely on its color name. Just as a paint company may have a dozen variations of white, each with a specific name, a yarn company with many colors has to come up with creative names, some of which may have little relation to the actual hues.

One company's "sapphire," for example, is actually an emerald green. Also, retail outlets that purchase yarns for resale sometimes change the original color names and color numbers that you may be accustomed to ordering.

A company that has been in business for many years producing yarns primarily for the textile industry may have a large assortment of colors available, having retained many similar colors that were the results of special orders. Most color lines are strong in certain hues and deficient in others. While companies with smaller color lines may offer some wonderful colors not available elsewhere, some lack a full spectrum of saturated hues. Only a few companies scientifically dye their yarns in specific increments based on a standard color system. Dye lot changes can produce noticeable differences in the same color.

Yarn sizes, such as 10/2 cotton, are supposed to be standards (in this example, 4,200 yards [3,840 m] per pound), but what is advertised as a particular size may vary from one company to another. Manufacturers do not always produce comparable products, so it's best to sample a brand before buying a large supply, and be cautious of judging luster from a small sample. Not all mercerized cotton in a particular size has the same luster or amount of twist. Excess twist not only makes it more difficult to put warp on the loom but also reduces the luster. Even from the same company, an occasional cone of yarn may have more twist because of technical malfunctions during the spinning or plying. The more you use a particular brand, the more familiar you will be with its normal qualities, and the more able you will be to recognize an aberration.

The texture of a yarn can influence the iridescence it produces. Some yarns incorporate plies of a different fiber, sometimes as "seeds" of a lustrous yarn that will enhance light reflection. A yarn with pronounced texture can interfere with reflection, however.

A Matter of Twist

The amount of twist in a yarn affects its luster because twist reduces reflection. Monofilament yarns are chemically extruded with little or no twist that would interfere with light reflection, so they tend to be very lustrous. Yarns spun from long fibers also tend to have more luster than short-staple yarns, partly because they require less twist to hold them together. Consequently, a balanced yarn plied from long-fibered singles will require even less ply twist and can be more lustrous than one composed of shorter fibers. The most lustrous silk and linen yarns are usually made from long-staple fibers.

While extra twist can reduce reflection, it can also add texture to fabric. A firmly twisted yarn can make a twill line stand out. In plain weave, a little extra twist in a yarn, combined with a sett that's open enough to allow some movement of yarn within the fabric, can result in a texture called *tracking*. Basically a "designer wrinkle," tracking happens when yarns within a fabric move as a unit, and it appears as intersecting diagonal lines that form attractive patterns. Like twill diagonals, these tiny ridges can help reflect light and enhance iridescence. The effect is usually not evident until the fabric is wet-finished.

Yarn twist is categorized by the apparent slant of the twist in the yarn. When you look at a strand held vertically, Z-twist yarn has a twist that appears slanted up toward the right, like the center stroke of the letter Z. In an S-twist yarn, the slant is up toward the left.

Most yarns are composed of twisted fibers and two or more plies, individual twisted strands (*singles*) that are then twisted together. The twist in the ply is normally the opposite direction of the twist in its component singles, although that's not always the case in complex novelty yarns plied in multiple stages. In general, the more plies a yarn has, or the more twist it has in its singles, the more twist it incorporates in the ply. Twist in a balanced plied yarn, however, is generally less than in its component singles. Multiple strands can be plied together in one step, or a yarn may be plied in more than one stage. The final twist in the yarn is the one to consider when planning your weaving.

Many yarns, both handspun and factory-spun, are spun with a Z twist and plied S. Most of my weaving yarns are S-plied, although I find more variation in linen yarns

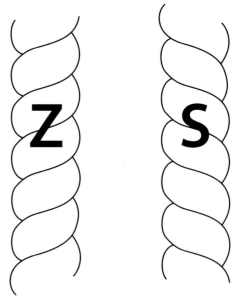

Z and S twists.

than in cotton, silk, wool, or rayon. Because unspun flax fiber tends to have a natural S twist, linen is often spun S and plied Z. Many sewing threads also tend to be spun S and plied Z.

It's easy to determine the twist direction of a thread, even if it's a very fine one and the twist is hard to see. Grasp a strand horizontally between your hands, and twist away from you (clockwise) with your right hand. If the yarn has an S twist, the twist will become tighter. If it has a Z twist, it will untwist.

Similar yarns from the same source tend to have the same twist direction and amount. However, not all yarns of the same type have the same characteristics, so it is a good idea to check. In mercerized cotton from North America, the ply direction varies from one brand to another, and combining different brands in the same project can give unexpected results. If you are working with warp and weft of the same type of yarn from the same source, both will probably have the same twist direction, and most often this will be an S ply.

Comments on Certain Fibers and Yarns

Cotton

Cotton is one of my favorite yarns for many purposes, from dish towels to clothing fabric. Cotton yarns come in many sizes and textures and are readily available from a number of sources. Cotton is usually classified as unmercerized or mercerized.

Unmercerized cotton is soft, with little or no luster, and relatively inexpensive. It requires strong color contrast to produce effective iridescence because of its lack of luster. Common sizes are 8/2, 16/2, and 20/2, the latter two most often as mill ends.

Mercerization is a chemical treatment primarily applied to cellulose yarns, especially cotton, but sometimes linen and hemp. Yarn is held under tension and treated with lye, then neutralized with acid. The process makes mercerized cotton yarn (often called pearl or perle cotton) smoother, stronger, easier to dye, and much more lustrous than untreated cotton yarn. The luster, ease of weaving, ease of care, and relative affordability make mercerized cotton an excellent choice for iridescent fabrics. It is commonly available in four sizes: 3/2, 5/2, 10/2, and 20/2.

My favorite yarn for lightweight clothing fabrics that are affordable and easy to care for is 20/2 pearl cotton. Unfortunately, the primary source for 20/2 pearl cotton in North America is no longer selling that size in dyed colors except black. A couple of other companies still offer 20/2 pearl cotton in a limited range of colors, and mercerized 16/2 cotton (available from at least one European source) can be a suitable substitute.

Linen

Linen comes in two main forms, *tow* and *line*. Tow linen is spun from shorter flax fibers and tends to be fuzzier and heavier. Line linen is the better quality yarn, spun from longer flax fibers. Consequently it has more luster, and it is the better choice for iridescence. Line linen is available in sizes ranging from relatively heavy yarns to very fine ones.

Linen is a strong yarn, so singles yarns are available and practical for fine fabric, especially for weft, and can have more luster than plied linen. Singles yarns also flatten more easily with a hard press, adding to their ability to reflect light. All linen is stronger wet than dry and is easier to weave in a humid climate. In a dry climate, spritzing the warp with water as you weave will help keep it from breaking.

Relatively fine yarns—10/1 or 20/2 and finer—can also be useful for open-weave fabrics, including double weave and other layered fabrics. Linen's stiffness makes it relatively stable at open setts, and it has been used this way traditionally for inlaid transparencies for many years. It is one of the more practical yarns for this purpose.

Most linen yarns come from European sources and are available from a few American companies in a range of colors. A few linen yarns are mercerized. *Cottolin* is a blend of cotton and linen and usually has less luster than pure linen.

Silk

Although there are slubby, dull silk yarns made from short fibers, weavers can also choose more lustrous yarns from a number of sources and in an excellent range of colors. Silk is expensive, and some companies sell it in relatively small quantities, making it more affordable to purchase in a variety of colors. Fine silk is always an excellent choice for iridescent clothing fabrics. It is strong and easy to weave, and a small amount of fine silk goes a long way.

Numerous sizes are available in plied silk yarns, the most practical sizes ranging from 20/2 (approximately the same diameter as 10/2 cotton) to 60/2. The finest and most lustrous is reeled silk, which is the most expensive and hardest to find. Spun silk is what most companies sell, most of which has very good luster. Almost all silk comes from Asia.

Wool

Although wool is often considered to have little luster, some types from sheep breeds with longer fibers have considerably more luster than others. Fiber from angora goats (mohair) and llamas, generically categorized as wool, can also produce yarns with good luster. You are more likely to find luster in wool yarns that are spun worsted-style rather than woolen-style. With most commercial wool and related yarns, a strong color contrast will give more opportunity for iridescence than analogous colors.

A recent introduction, particularly in knitting yarns, is mercerized wool. Mercerization adds loft, strength, and some luster to certain yarns, and some commercial brands are said to produce good iridescence. A color contrast is probably beneficial and may have more effect than the mercerization process itself. The mercerized wool I have examined does not impress me as having much luster, and it is more expensive than other wool yarns.

Rayon

Rayon, a man-made fiber created from cellulose, was first invented as an inexpensive substitute for silk because of its high luster. There are several types, of which viscose rayon is probably the most common. There are several rayon yarns on the market for weavers, and fine rayon mill ends are sometimes available from some sources. While some of the newer rayons are touted as "environmentally friendly" because they come from renewable sources or waste materials, all are chemically extruded products that have little resemblance to their source materials.

Among the newer rayons is *lyocell*, sold under the trade name Tencel. Tencel has become very popular with weavers because of its high luster, ease of weaving, and the pleasing hand of the fabric. The color selection, in 8/2 yarns (interchangeable with 10/2 cotton), is good but limited and does not currently include saturated green or saturated yellow. The yarn tends to be more expensive than mercerized cotton. A former supplier of dyed 10/2 and 20/2 Tencel has ceased manufacturing it, and 20/2 Tencel is currently available only in white or as custom-dyed yarns.

Bamboo yarn is available in 8/2 and 16/2 sizes, comparable to the same sizes of cotton. The most readily available bamboo yarn is a type of rayon with a high luster and comes in a limited color range. It has become popular with weavers and can produce excellent iridescence.

It is a very slick yarn that needs to be woven closely for stability; with normal setts for its size, I find the fabric to have more drape than I want. Increasingly, yarn spun from bamboo fiber, rather than chemically processed, is becoming available.

Soy silk, made from soybeans, and *Ingeo*, from corn, are other synthetic yarns that are not widely available but can be obtained from some sources. Many commercial iridescent fabrics contain additional synthetics, such as polyester and polypropylene.

Chenille

Chenille is available in cotton, rayon, silk, and occasionally other fibers. It is a woven yarn, cut from fabric parallel to warps that are spaced very closely at intervals to hold the weft stable when it's cut. Because the cut fibers stick out in every direction, they diffuse light and don't

An attempt to mimic velvet by crossing two colors of rayon chenille produced a fabric that is not iridescent, despite the split-complementary colors.

produce uniform reflection. The cut pile also tends to absorb light. These characteristics make it unsuitable for effective iridescence, especially when both warp and weft are chenille.

Sewing Thread

Sewing threads come in a wide selection of colors, sizes, and fiber content. They are easy to use as weft, and some come on narrow spools that will fit on a boat shuttle. Sewing thread is more challenging to use as warp, but it is not beyond the capability of many weavers to do so. Heavier sewing threads are comparable to some other fine weaving yarns, such as 20/2 cotton, at similar setts.

A few years ago, after having woven at 60 and 80 ends per inch for special projects, I challenged myself to weave at 120 e.p.i. with sewing-thread warp. I bought a spool of quilting thread, since it came on a large enough package that I didn't need to buy multiple spools for a small sample. I put on a narrow warp, only a few inches wide, and used a finer, more lustrous sewing thread as weft, in a contrasting color.

To my surprise, I wasn't able to weave plain weave; 120 e.p.i. was much too close. With difficulty, I wove a small sample of a very steep 2/2 twill, but it was impossible to make a balanced weave no matter how hard I beat, and iridescence was subdued. I hadn't done an inch wrapping ahead of time to test the sett, and I had not paid attention to how much the size of sewing threads can vary.

I respaced the warp at 60 e.p.i. instead of 120, which proved perfect for a balanced 2/2 twill that would make a lovely iridescent clothing fabric. It was still too close for plain weave, which might have worked at 45 to 48 e.p.i. . . . similar to setts I've used frequently with yarns such as 20/2 cotton for twills.

Most sewing threads are quite strong; those spun from cotton are usually mercerized, which adds luster and strength. Many sewing threads are available in synthetic fibers with extreme luster, metallic sheen, or fibers that reflect multiple colors. Using sewing thread in combination with a heavier yarn can be effective in producing iridescent satin/sateen, and a heavier yarn can help subdue a strong value contrast in the fine thread.

Very fine synthetic threads, such as some rayon, may be very slick and difficult to warp with. Misting threads that are prone to static charge can help tame them. I found it necessary to tape down rayon thread as soon as I sleyed a reed, to keep it from slipping back out.

There is only a hint of iridescence in this twill fabric, which was woven at too close a sett.

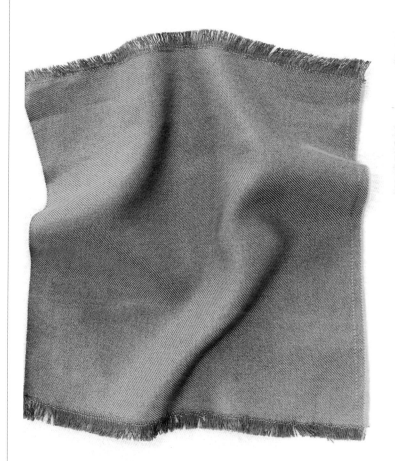

Quilting thread at 60 e.p.i. made a good warp for a 2/2 twill fabric with wonderful drape, woven with a finer sewing thread for weft.

Ribbon

Because ribbon is flat, a shiny ribbon can be an excellent reflector of light, and weaving with ribbon can produce wonderful iridescence. It is available in a virtually unlimited range of colors and many widths and made of many different substances, ranging from woven fabrics in natural yarns to plastics.

Keeping ribbon flat while you weave can be a challenge; the flatter it remains in the fabric, the better it will reflect light. Most weavers use ribbon as an accent, rather than as the main component of a fabric.

Nylon Monofilament

Nylon monofilament is not often thought of as yarn, but more often as fishing line, in which form it is most readily available. It is stiff enough to be relatively stable at a very open sett and, sold as fishing line, comes in several sizes. The finer sizes are most suitable for weaving, and the colors and uses are limited.

Wire

Although relatively few weavers work with metal wire, fine wire can be woven like yarn on a loom and is very strong. It's stable at an open sett and is malleable, so it can be shaped for three-dimensional artwork. Anodized copper wire has become popular with bead workers and is usually available on small spools in a good range of colors. I prefer to use 30-gauge wire for weaving. The wire is very lustrous and relatively expensive.

Anodized copper wire comes in many colors.

The New Yarns

In recent years, threads that darken or change color in sunlight have come on the market. The earlier threads came in four colors, which intensified in sunlight and returned to their pastel tints indoors. Now there are white threads that turn certain colors in the sun and quickly return to white out of sunlight. The change can happen thousands of times, but continued exposure to sunlight will reduce the fabric's ability to change color. Colors are more intense in cool climates than in warm ones. Since the color-changing material is transparent, colors are not saturated. The range of colors is being expanded to at least a couple dozen.

Most of these photochromic threads, so far, are too fine to be useful to many weavers. However, knitters can now find sport-weight yarns that change from white to colors (the first on the market turn pink or purple in sunlight). The ones I sampled are white wool wrapped closely with fine polypropylene, the synthetic thread that reacts to ultraviolet light. Although of limited use to weavers because of its relatively large size, it is strong and has little stretch, making it easy to weave. The polypropylene is a shiny thread that adds luster to the yarn. The pale colors are of limited effectiveness for good iridescence, at least with currently available yarns.

As more of these yarns come on the market, they may become available in more colors and more sizes (and, perhaps, at less expense). Since knitters are the primary market for most new yarns, it remains to be seen how useful these yarns will be for weavers, but the potential ability for sunlight to make a white fabric into an iridescent one is intriguing.

There is a host of newer yarns that mimic natural iridescence by reflecting a full spectrum of colors. Many of these contain Mylar, a plastic polyester film (polyethylene). These are used extensively in fabrics for formal wear and are also available as yarns for weaving. These are often called *holographic* yarns, which is technically inaccurate. (A hologram is an image that appears three-dimensional, the result of a particular method of photographing the light reflected from an object.)

Retroreflective yarns have tiny glass beads glued to them that reflect light intensely, and the yarns are available in different sizes. Those I've examined are dull gray until seen at a certain angle. These are the same beads used on road signs, road stripes, and reflective clothing worn by bikers and others who need to be visible in the dark. It might be possible to incorporate these in handwoven fabrics that will look dull at certain angles and flash a

These white yarns become colorful (pink or purple) when exposed to sunlight. The change from white to colored is rapid and can be repeated many times. This twill sample crossing pink and purple yarns is not particularly iridescent because of the pale colors.

brilliant light at others, perhaps giving or enhancing an iridescent effect.

Many iridescent commercial fabrics incorporate metallics, which reflect light very well. Merely including metallic yarn does not guarantee iridescence, but it certainly enhances the effect, and a little bit goes a long way. Lurex is a brand with brilliant luster in quite a few colors.

While most so-called metallic yarn is actually plastic, it is possible to buy fine metallic yarns, made from real metal and suitable for weaving, from a few specialty suppliers. These most often are copper or stainless steel, and they can create a harsh fabric that creases readily (but may have possibilities for three-dimensional artwork). Some of these are now available combined with fibers such as silk. Some sources offer other exotic threads in addition to true metallics, some plied with different colors for an iridescent effect in a single thread. Many of these specialty threads are from Japan, known for its innovative new textiles.

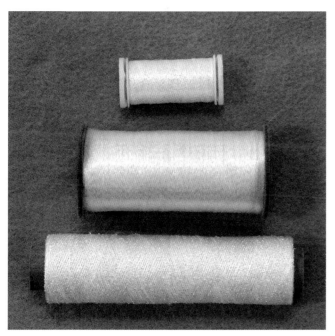

Mylar yarns reflect a rainbow of colors and come in several tints and sizes.

Yarns that reflect more than one color are available from specialty suppliers.

The Influence of Weave Structure

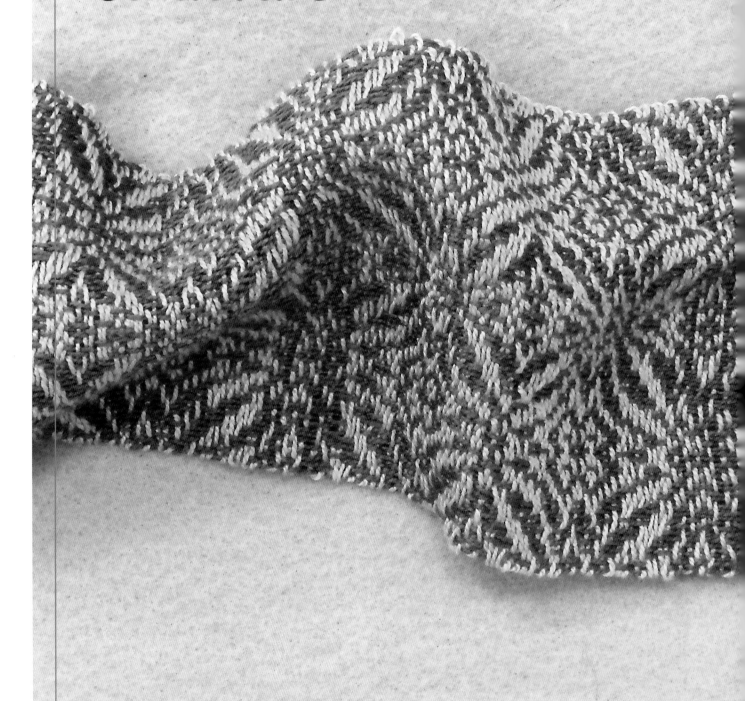

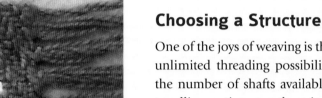

CHAPTER SIX

Choosing a Structure

One of the joys of weaving is that we have almost unlimited threading possibilities (expanded by the number of shafts available) and even more treadling options, so there is always something new to try and no excuse to get bored! This also makes it challenging to predict which weave structures will produce iridescence and which will not, and any rule you come up with is likely to have exceptions. Many other factors are involved besides weave structure, including relative thread size, sett, beat, luster, color choice, and relative value, and changing one factor affects others. However, there are certain features that can enhance the effect and others that tend to discourage it. You can weave beautiful iridescent fabrics on only two shafts, in plain weave or basketweave. Or you can add as many additional shafts as you have available, perhaps taking advantage of a dobby or jacquard loom.

A study of factory-woven fabrics reveals myriad effective weave structures, ranging from plain weave to jacquard-woven brocades or satin stripes on a plain-weave ground. In some cases, the patterning is independent of an iridescent ground and forms an attractive accent on the surface.

This factory-woven jacquard fabric is iridescent in three colors, particularly the blue and orange.

Twill Weaves

Many twills and twill-based weaves are good choices, especially if they have strong diagonal pattern lines or create blocks that reflect light uniformly.

Plaited twills, although not always balanced, show the intersection of warp and weft diagonals and often feature

A balanced 2/2 twill produces good iridescence in contrasting colors.

planes of reflection, as well as having the benefit of patterns that themselves look interwoven. Point twills can produce intersecting diagonal patterns that reflect light differently at different angles.

Some of my favorite twill variations are crêpe weaves (not to be confused with crumply crêpe *fabrics* from yarn with extra twist). Although not a distinct weave structure, crêpes are fabrics with an overall mottled effect, which are often broken twills. The less distinct the pattern, the "better" a crêpe is said to be. (I prefer those with attractive patterns!) Even a patterned crêpe often has an indistinct pattern as you're weaving it, and the pattern is more obvious viewed at an angle, or after the fabric is wet-finished. The allure of a pattern that appears and disappears, combined with color that comes and goes, has great appeal!

Crêpe weaves can be defined in the threading or treadling or both. Broken twill threadings create crêpes if

The iridescence in *Oruru River Mudflats* by Agnes Hauptli is striking in three shades/tints of bronze for warp, crossed with blue weft. Silk, 32 shafts; advancing twill threading, twill treadling to produce a curved design. Photo courtesy of Agnes Hauptli.

treadled as a straight twill, or as drawn in. A straight draw threading can be treadled as a broken twill. On four shafts, I make my own variations using 2/2 twill picks plus plain-weave picks. If the threading is a broken twill, true plain weave is not possible, but the standard 1+3 or 2+4 treadlings add to the pattern interest.

The Influence of Twist in Twill Fabric

Although often overlooked by weavers, twist can be a factor in designing effective fabrics, including iridescent ones. The twist of warp and weft yarns influences the appearance of a finished fabric, particularly when woven in straight twill, with diagonals that slant up to the left (S twill) or up to the right (Z twill). The twill direction can be determined in the threading or in the treadling, so a twill threaded in one direction can be treadled in the opposite order to create the opposite diagonal as desired. A twill fabric has a warp diagonal and a weft diagonal (viewed with the weft vertical, turned 90 degrees from the warp) in the opposite direction.

Warp and weft yarns with the same twist direction (either S or Z) tend to fit together closer than yarns of opposite twist, and this creates a flatter fabric with weave structure that may be subdued. This will normally be the situation if you're crossing different colors of the same type and size of yarn, from the same company. However, there are ways to make a twill line more obvious even when warp and weft twist are the same.

Extra twist helps make a twill line stand out. A closer sett, longer floats, or using a heavier yarn with firm twist can also make a twill line more prominent. A compressed twill (more picks per inch than warp ends per inch) will accentuate a weft twill line.

Choosing which twill line to make more distinct can be important when working with value contrast. Choosing a darker warp and accentuating the warp twill line

These 4-shaft crêpes have effective iridescence, look more complex than they are, and drape beautifully for apparel.

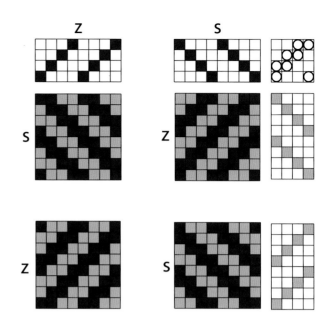

Twill direction in threading and treadling

may help keep a lighter weft from overpowering the warp, or you can make a darker weft more dominant by choosing a twill direction that accents it. When you want both warp and weft to have equal play, perhaps when working with colors of about the same value, you have options to make either twill prominent or dampen the appearance of the structure.

Striped Fabrics

Multicolored stripes in warp or weft can produce the effect of space-dyed yarn and make effective iridescence, particularly if the changing colors are within a limited color family. For best results, the colors should change

IIIIIIIIIIIIIIIIIIIIIIIIIIIIIIIIIIIIIIIIIIIIIIIIIIIIIIIIIIIIIIIIIIIIIII

If warp and weft have the same twist, make the warp twill line stand out with a twill line opposite the yarn twist.

    S warp, S weft, Z twill

    Z warp, Z weft, S twill

If warp and weft have the same twist, make the weft line stand out with a twill line the same as the yarn twist.

    S warp, S weft, S twill

    Z warp, Z weft, Z twill

If warp and weft twist are opposite, make a twill more distinct using the same twill line as the weft twist.

    S warp, Z weft, Z twill

    Z warp, S weft, S twill

If warp and weft twist are opposite, dampen the twill effect using the same twill line as the warp twist.

    S warp, Z weft, S twill

    Z warp, S weft, Z twill

(Information adapted from Mary Elizabeth Laughlin, *More Than Four: A Book for Multiple Harness Weavers*, Robin and Russ Handweavers, 1976.)

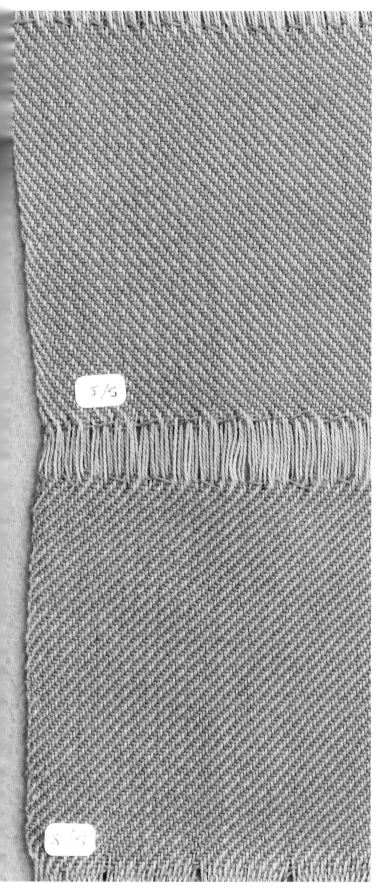

S twill (top, left slant) and Z twill (bottom, right slant).

very frequently to keep stripes to just one or two adjacent threads of the same color.

As mentioned earlier, alternating warp colors on different shafts, or weft colors on successive picks, produces a striped fabric that may have a hint of iridescence, if there is strong color contrast, but this is usually not effective. Since the colors are crossed by different threads with each pick, the reflection off the threads is broken up. Twill, with floats, may be more successful than plain weave.

Shadow weave alternates colors in the warp on different shafts, as well as on alternating picks in the weft. Because light reflection is interrupted when different threads cross on successive picks, shadow weave tends not to be iridescent. Log cabin, another color-and-weave effect, gives similar results. I have used it successfully to accentuate particular colors when working with multiple warp or weft colors functioning together.

When fabrics with wider stripes are pleated parallel to the stripes, they can become quite iridescent. The texture of pleating transforms the fabric because it produces planes of reflection.

Pile, Lace, and Supplementary-Thread Weaves

Pile weaves normally hide their backgrounds and are not good choices for iridescence . . . yet there are iridescent velvets. The same is true of supplemental weft (or warp) weaves with floats, especially if the pattern yarn is heavier than the background yarn. Floats of lace, overshot, and Ms & Os tend to group together to hide backgrounds.

Weaves such as (American) honeycomb can be used to outline cells of finer yarns in contrasting colors, again adding an attractive texture without contributing to background iridescence. (In Europe, "honeycomb" is the name given to American waffle weaves . . . which may have some possibilities for iridescence.)

Balanced Weaves

When you're crossing threads of different colors, balanced weaves are good options, since they allow the colors to show equally. This does not require plain weave . . . in fact, plain-weave fabrics include tapestry and other variations where either the warp or weft is all or mostly hidden. A 2/2 twill is often called a *balanced twill* because it passes over two ends and under the next two uniformly. However, this can also result in a warp-faced or weft-faced fabric, depending on sett, yarn size, and beat. A heavy warp crossed with a fine weft may show a 45-degree twill angle usually associated with balanced weaves, yet not be balanced in terms of sett, beat, and thread size.

Unbalanced Weaves

Weft-faced weaves (such as bound weave, tapestry, and sateen), and warp-faced weaves (including rep weave and satin, along with combinations such as damask) are not normally iridescent. There are some exceptions, however. You can, for example, weave iridescent threads into your tapestries. And there are some spectacularly iridescent satins.

Unbalanced twills, such as 3/1 and 1/3 twills, are not always effective for iridescence because they are warp-dominant on one face and weft-dominant on the other. A strong color or value contrast can create some iridescent effects, particularly if the warmer and/or lighter color is the one that shows least. You might also choose a heavier yarn for the color that shows less, to make it stand out more.

Other warp-dominant and weft-dominant weaves that allow the cross threads to show can be iridescent. Echo weave, turned taqueté, and others have a denser warp than weft; a heavier weft yarn is sometimes used to better balance the warp.

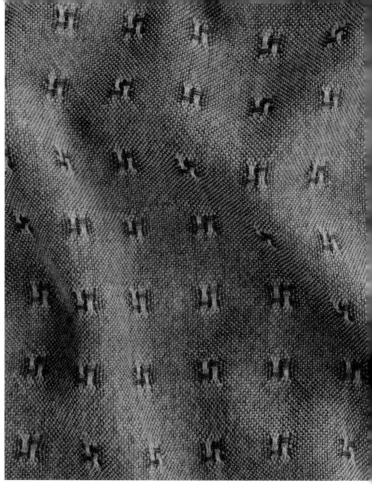

The floats on this fabric (4-shaft huck, turned spots) produce texture on an iridescent background.

This overshot scarf has a contrasting pattern yarn the same size as the background yarns, beaten gently enough that it shows some color shifting at different angles. Scarf courtesy of the Arizona Federation of Weavers and Spinners Guilds/Fibers Through Time conference.

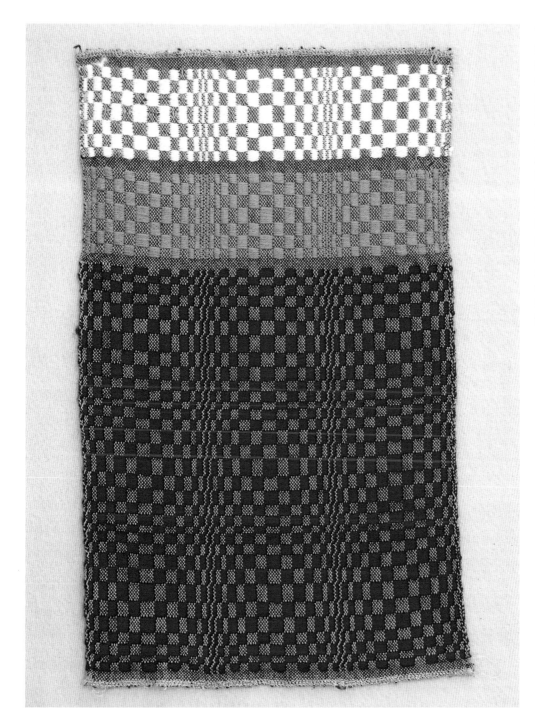

This overshot sampler, with warp and tabby in different colors of 10/2 cotton, plus a heavier pattern yarn, has an iridescent background. The pattern, which is not itself iridescent, forms a texture on the surface. Where I used a red pattern weft, you notice more of the blue in the background. A blue pattern weft accents the red in the background. A neutral (white) pattern weft shows off an equal balance of warp and tabby colors.

Echo

In recent years, echo effects (parallel threadings in different colors) have become very popular among weavers, particularly those with eight or more shafts to play with. While not a distinct weave structure, echo is a color and threading technique that works with several weaves. Echo fabrics are often warp-dominant, and a contrasting weft (sometimes heavier) can provide good iridescence.

Modern echo weaves, which can be woven on as few as four shafts, often use two colors in the warp, with each threading line a different color, and a third color in the weft. Especially with eight or more shafts, patterns are typically curved, with feathered edges, and additional parallel threadings and colors are popular. Marian Stubenitsky has specialized in achieving spectacular iridescent effects with more colors and multiple parallel threadings that are closer together than commonly seen. In her book samples, she uses four or eight colors in her warps, with as many as eight colors on as few as eight shafts.

This unbalanced 3/1 twill exhibits a hint of iridescence.

The puckered stripes of structural seersucker are not iridescent, although the background crossing the same contrasting colors is. The stripes form a texture on an iridescent background.

Inspired by the colors in an oil slick, Agnes Hauptli's scarf has a networked echo threading on 20 shafts, with rust and purple warp, 60/2 silk sett at 72 e.p.i. The green weft is 140/2 silk, and the treadling is a twill variation. Photo courtesy of Agnes Hauptli.

This 8-shaft echo scarf has blue warps echoed by green warps on higher shafts. The magenta weft provides iridescence. 8/2 Tencel sett at 42 e.p.i.

This 12-shaft echo fabric by Marian Stubenitsky, in 20/2 mercerized cotton, displays beautiful iridescence. There are four warp colors: purple, orange, green, and blue, each used twice, and an advancing twill treadling with almost two thousand picks in a repeat. The weft is a red-violet alpaca yarn, much thicker than the warp. Photo by Joke van den Broek, courtesy of Marian Stubenitsky.

On 32 shafts with eight warp colors and a dark blue weft, this echo scarf glows with changing colors. Photo by Fried Kampes, courtesy of Marian Stubenitsky.

Alice Schlein introduced the term *echo weave* (*Weaver's*, Summer 1996, Issue 32) for color variations on parallel threadings, in networked twills. Most modern references to echo weave refer to her techniques. In the 1930s, Bertha Needham used the same name for another color effect in simpler weaves (often twill-based), where, for example, one color is used for a particular twill pick and a second color, often a shade or tint of the first, follows on the next higher twill pick. The color changes are in the weft.

Bonnie Inouye's 24-shaft echo scarf, *Plumage*, has two layers of warp in green Tencel and several blues (cotton and Tencel). A slightly finer weft consists of three strands of fine silk and cotton in reds and red-orange. Photo courtesy of Bonnie Inouye.

Turned Taqueté

Another warp-dominant weave, turned taqueté is popular and can be woven on certain double weave threadings. It typically incorporates two warp colors and a contrasting weft that is sometimes a little finer than the warps. Turned taqueté can be woven on as few as four shafts.

Double Weave

Double weave with contrasting warps and wefts can produce wonderful iridescence in some cases, depending on the variation, color order, and treadlings. Marian Stubenitsky has popularized double weaves with four colors (two each in warp and weft) on as few as four shafts, and more complex versions incorporating more colors. She uses parallel threadings and networked

pattern lines. Her double weaves have integrated as well as separate-layer sections (pocket weave), and the fabrics are iridescent wherever there is strong color contrast between warp and weft, and the colors are of similar value.

Complex Weaves

A number of years ago, an American group called Cross Country Weavers did a study on iridescent fabrics. I was privileged to see the samples, briefly, and as befits that experienced group, many of the swatches were quite complex fabrics woven on many shafts. My first impression was that some samples weren't as iridescent as I might have expected. (In retrospect, perhaps the examples that I found disappointing suffered from too much value contrast.) It did make me wonder if it's possible to make a fabric so complex that it dampens out the effect of iridescence.

That theory seems plausible. Someone in a class likened such a fabric to a crystal with many faces, or a gemstone with many facets, both of which would scatter light in too many directions. Gem cutters have adopted standard procedures to make distinct planes that produce the best reflection. I have heard that the crystal orb that forms the royal scepter in London is so completely facetted that it is not as brilliant as it might be.

Accomplishing such a feat—designing a fabric so complex that, based on various factors, it should be iridescent but isn't—is not something easy to do. It would probably need to have no threading or treadling repeats that would create obvious pattern repeats that would reflect light. Still, such a fabric might be no more effective than plain weave at discouraging iridescence. My experiments with a 12-shaft crêpe pattern and a 12-pick treadling sequence gave an attractive fabric with a discernible design, and it was quite iridescent both with contrasting warp and weft and also with analogous colors. I've given up on this challenge and have decided to be satisfied that there are so many ways I *can* achieve iridescence!

Sedona, an award-winning shawl by Bonnie Inouye in turned taqueté, was woven on 24 shafts with two warp layers, one of which is hand dyed in warm hues. The weft is finer than the warp. Photo courtesy of Bonnie Inouye.

This turned taqueté fabric, designed and woven by Cynthia Broughton, has blue and green warps of 20/2 mercerized cotton. A finer orange weft of 40/2 cotton provides a touch of iridescence. 16 shafts, 60 e.p.i. Sample courtesy of Cynthia Broughton.

Cynthia Broughton designed and wove this four-color double weave with blue and green warps and red and light blue wefts in 20/2 mercerized cotton on 16 shafts. Iridescence is evident where red and green threads intersect. The threading is the same as in photo above, but with a sett of 45 e.p.i. Sample courtesy of Cynthia Broughton.

This 12-shaft fabric in two colorways is iridescent despite a pattern that appears indistinct in a drawdown.

Pattern of the fabric in photo at left, (Fig. 876 from G. H. Oelsner, *A Handbook of Weaves*, Dover reprint, 1952.)

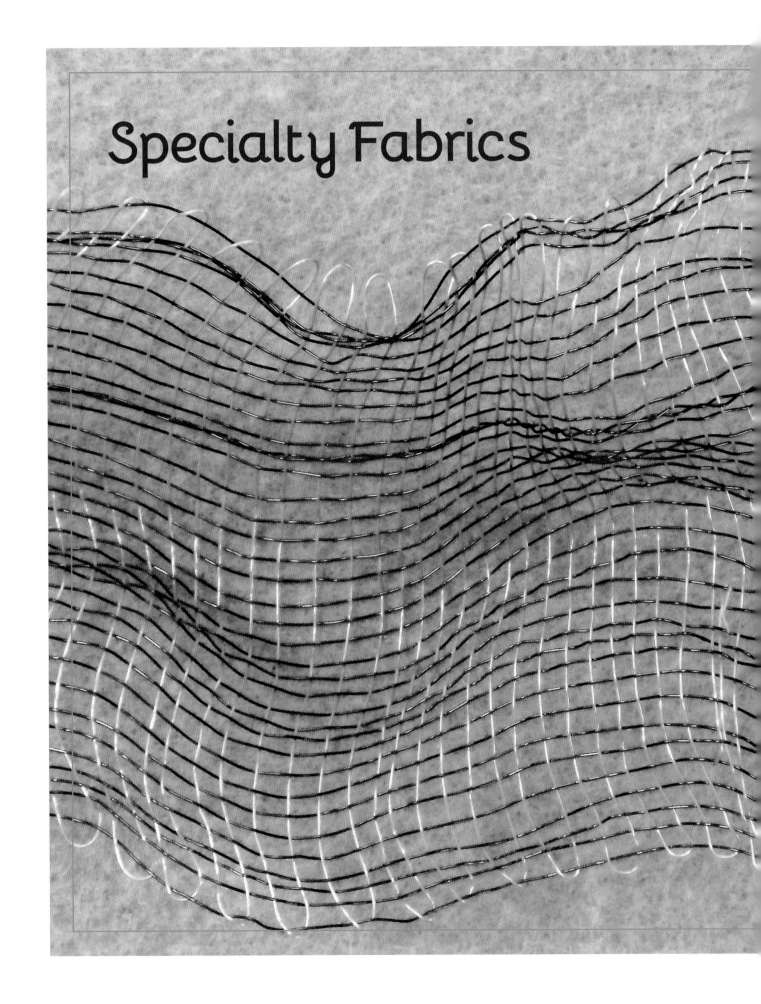

Specialty Fabrics

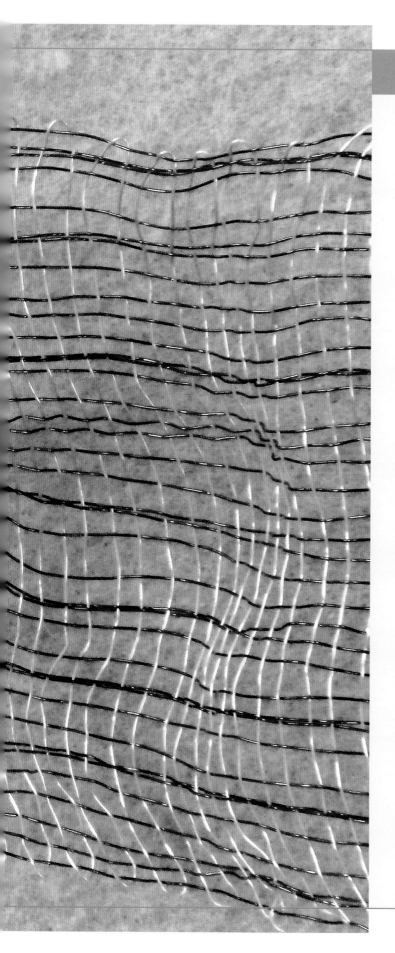

CHAPTER SEVEN

Sheer Fabrics

Fine transparent or translucent fabrics that are iridescent, even though they appear to be mostly air, seem especially magical. Light passes through them as well as reflecting from them in their component colors. A typical commercial fabric of this type is woven with threads finer than a human hair (300 wraps [2.5 cm] per inch, or more) but has an open plain-weave structure, with a sett of 60 to 80 ends per inch. Many of these threads are apparently sized to make them stiffer in the open weave and easier to handle. Working with threads so fine they are barely visible is more of a challenge than many handweavers want to attempt.

Fortunately, there are ways of producing airy fabrics using heavier materials and coarser setts. These include lace weaves and open double- or single-layer weaves, and working with stiff materials such as linen, wire, and monofilament nylon.

Lace Weaves

Leno, a lace weave traditionally worked by hand by twisting adjacent warps or groups of warps, can be woven with loom-controlled twisting in a variation called *bead* or *doup* leno, using as few as four shafts. This creates an open-weave fabric quickly and easily that will be warp-dominant.

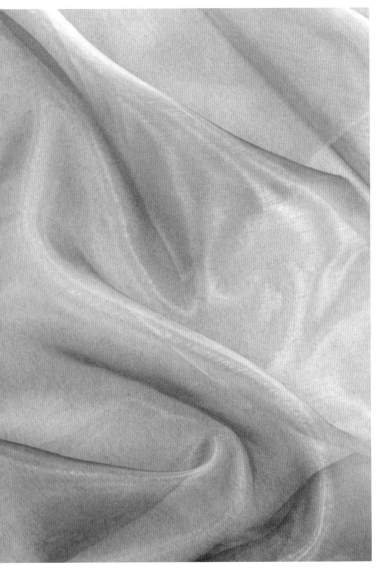

Iridescence is striking in this sample of a commercial fabric that's almost invisible.

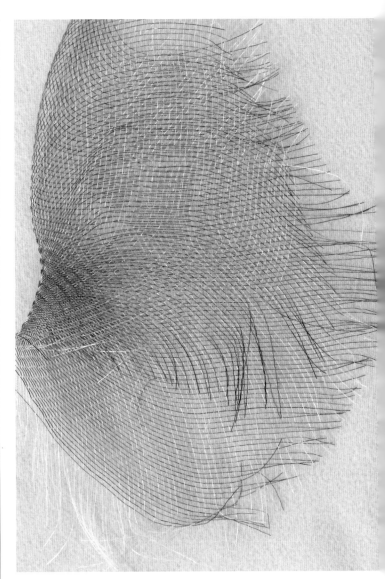

This commercial nylon monofilament fabric crosses complements of red-violet and yellow-green and is markedly iridescent.

A contrasting weft can produce subtle iridescence, since there is considerably more warp than weft in the fabric, and using a bouclé yarn or another textured weft will help stabilize the structure. Because the twist must change direction with every pick, the reflection from the warp is muted.

You can weave huck on four or more shafts as turned spots with contrasting warp and weft on a plain-weave ground (see Huck Yardage, pages 128–129). While the floats do not appear to shift color, they provide an attractive texture on an iridescent background. When you notice the warp floats primarily, it is the contrasting weft color that stands out in the background. When the weft

floats seem more prominent, the warp color is more obvious in the plain weave.

In general, lace weaves do not create good iridescence by themselves because the floats tend to pack together. An open, lacy fabric might be effective as an overlay for another fabric in a different color. Even plain weave, crammed and spaced at intervals, might allow an underlayer to show through and create some iridescence.

Weaving with Monofilament Nylon

The floral industry has, in recent years, produced crisp open-weave nylon (or other synthetic) fabrics used to stiffen floral arrangements. Called floral wrap, this

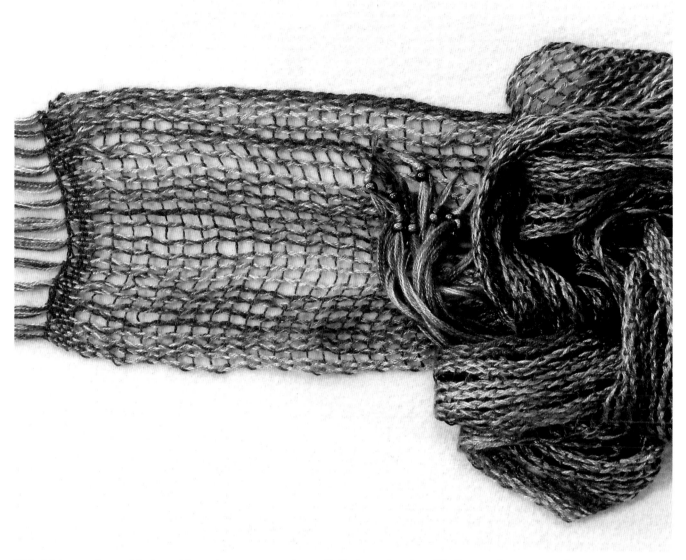

This iridescent scarf in bead leno has a magenta weft that contrasts with the cooler warp colors.

material comes in a variety of colorways, some of which are iridescent. The natural luster of the nylon also enhances iridescence; the monofilament thread has no twist to dampen the effect.

Handweavers can make similar fabrics with nylon fishing line, as I have done when designing layered transparencies (open-weave fabrics with inlaid patterns). The fabric has limited uses, but it can be interesting for achieving the effect of sheer and layered fabrics in a practical-sized "yarn." Like weavings with wire, this stuff has sculptural possibilities for three-dimensional artwork.

Monofilament fishing line comes in a variety of colors (most often blue and clear, but also yellow, yellow-green, green, and red) in a variety of diameters. It is sold by "test weight," the theoretical weight of a fish you can catch on

the line without it breaking. Unfortunately, test weight is not standardized with respect to diameter, so some line in the same test is heavier than others. I've found that the least expensive line in a 6- or 8-pound test, with 100 or more wraps per inch (2.5 cm), weaves well at 12 e.p.i. An appropriate sett is approximately one-quarter to one-third of the normal plain-weave sett figured as half the number of wraps in an inch (2.5 cm). A 20-pound line can work well at 5 to 6 ends and picks per inch, for heavier installations.

The more exotic colors tend to be expensive and may not come in the same weights as the least expensive fishing line. Since nylon takes dye readily, you can easily dye inexpensive clear fishing line any color you wish. The color you see on a spool is greatly diluted when the

Working with Fishing Line

The most challenging aspect to working with fishing line is warping the loom. This stiff and wiry material is impossible to handle when wound in normal fashion on a warping board . . . it curls on itself as soon as tension is released. Weavers with sectional warp beams may be able to wind directly off the original spools under adequate tension. Lacking a sectional beam, I've measured two-warp-length sections on a warping board and then put them on the loom a pair of warps at a time. It's not necessary to use a hook at any stage because it's a stiff material. Start at the front of the loom, sley one end through the reed and a heddle, pass it around the back rod and back through the next heddle and dent. Even up the ends, and tape the pair temporarily and securely to the front beam. Proceed with each pair individually.

While this sounds tedious, it doesn't take long at 12 e.p.i. to sley and thread a warp of modest width. I recommend short warps, no longer than four yards (3.7 m), on a loom with good distance between front and back beams. This makes the warp pairs easier to manage and helps prevent permanent kinking of the warp and fabric as it winds around the warp and cloth beams, both of which need to be well padded. To help minimize distortion, I place terry-cloth towels between the fabric and the front beam and around the cloth beam. The loops in the towels fill in and help stabilize the open weave structure. I use only plain weave for this material, again to maximize stability in what is otherwise an unstable fabric.

Tying on to the front rod is tricky because fishing line is said to hold knots only when you're fishing and don't want it to! I tie one-inch (2.5 cm) bouts in double overhand knots and lace/lash the warp onto the rod. An angler's trick is to dampen the line while tying the knots.

Weaving with fishing line is different from weaving with yarn, but it's not difficult. Using a long stick shuttle (as close to the width of the warp as possible) lets you measure the monofilament as you wind it and avoids curls and kinks from winding onto a bobbin. Since this is not a fast technique, the stick shuttle does not significantly slow the weaving. It's important to wind enough on the shuttle to complete the entire panel you are working on, since overlapping the nylon to start a new strand is unlikely to be secure. Estimate the amount needed by multiplying the width by the picks per inch (e.g., 12 p.p.i.) by the length. Add enough for firmly woven hems, at least an inch for turning the ends under. These hems may require 100 picks per inch. Since the more closely woven areas tend to pull in more than the open weave, allow a bit of an angle for the weft in the shed, although not enough to leave loops at the selvedges. Pull the shuttle through, close the shed, and finish pulling the weft through on a closed shed. Press with the beater to space the wefts closely, but don't use a firm beat.

Although the wiry weft tends to bounce back when you try to beat it, the next row automatically aligns with the previous row. When weaving the open area, use a very low angle or arc in the shed to avoid loops at the selvedges. Use the same technique that you use for hems, adjusting the weft on a closed shed. Change sheds, then use the beater very gently to carefully space the rows.

Firmly woven hems stabilize the open fabric. Temporarily stabilize the ends with tape, then machine sew across the ends with "invisible" thread and turn them under immediately after removing the work from the loom, creasing them by hand. (An iron or a bag sealer will melt the nylon and make a mess of things!) As an alternative, it may be possible to sew across the open-weave area with close stitching and then bind the raw edge with a strip of clear plastic, folded over the edge and sewn on by machine after cutting off the closely woven hem. For either method, use close machine stitching and "invisible" sewing thread.

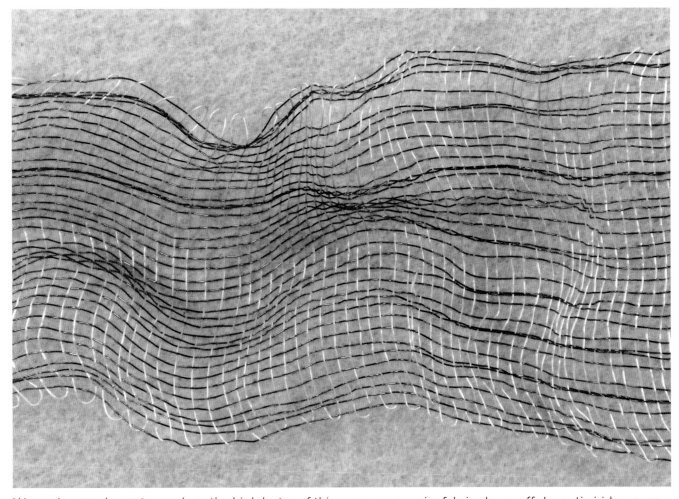

Woven in complementary colors, the high luster of this open-weave wire fabric shows off dramatic iridescence.

strands are spaced apart, so dyeing intense colors may give you the most satisfying results.

Weaving with Wire

Fine wire can be woven on a loom with open plain weave. Anodized copper wire, popular among bead workers, comes in many brilliant colors and can produce spectacular iridescence. Small spools are available from hobby suppliers, and larger quantities can be found online. I prefer a 30-gauge wire, which I can put on my loom using steel or wire heddles (string or Texsolv heddles might be cut by the wire) and single-sleying a reed for a sett of 12 e.p.i. The warping process is similar to working with monofilament nylon, starting at the front and wrapping the wire around the back rod and back to the front. For a small project, you may be able to wind a continuous warp right on the loom, rather than cutting each pair of warps before you start.

You can open sheds and weave and beat as if it were yarn. A stick shuttle may be most practical to minimize curls and kinks. Plain weave will be most stable, although wire is stiff enough that twills should also work well. Because of few intersections per inch, and the lack of elasticity in the wire, you don't need to allow much extra weft in the shed. Pull the weft snugly to minimize loops at the selvedges, and weave almost straight across. Like monofilament nylon, wire is most appropriate for artistic purposes, and it is more practical than nylon because the finished product is quite stable and can be bent into sculptural forms and changed as desired. Interestingly, some iridescent ribbon is woven with very fine wire so it can hold desired shapes.

Contrasting warp and weft colors can be dramatic in a single layer, or you can weave separate layers in single colors to create the effect of a sheer double fabric. Two different colors in each layer could be very dramatic.

Use heavy cardboard tubes, slit lengthwise, to protect front and back beams from being gouged by the wire. Use wire cutters to remove the woven piece from the loom and pliers to fold ends under, or perhaps a transparent binding to secure the cut and folded edges.

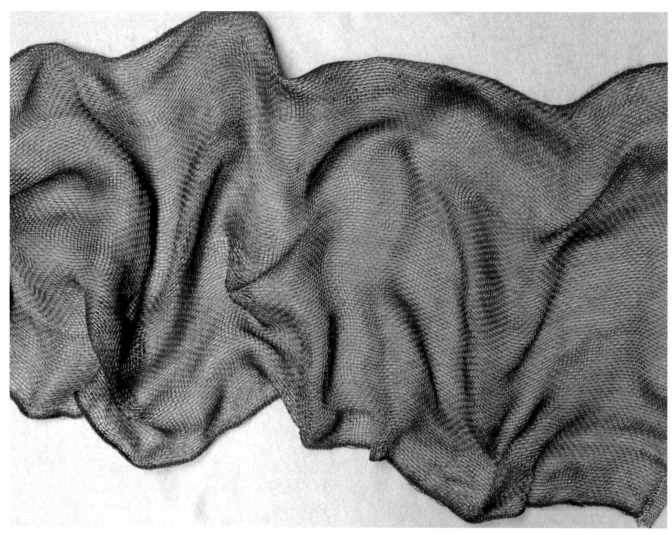

Woven as separate layers connected at the sides, this 4-shaft double weave glows in four colors: blue, green, orange, and yellow.

Layered Fabrics

Sheer double weave and other open fabrics with separate layers, with or without loom-controlled stitching, can create iridescence if it's possible to see a lower layer through an upper one. Putting a warm, high-value color such as yellow in the bottom layer will help it show through. If the fabric is reversed, that same color may overwhelm darker and cooler colors below and may not be as effective.

Moiré Effects

Traditional moiré (watered) silk and other fabrics are usually mechanically produced by pressing together fabric layers with ribbed rollers to produce a wavy pattern. Verda Elliott introduced how to weave moiré patterns ("Woven Moiré," *Weaver's*, Issue 20, 1993, pp. 38–43). I find it intriguing that the weaving patterns are devised in

much the same way as natural moiré patterns develop—by overlapping grids (twill patterns, usually different ones) at an angle not exceeding 45 degrees, then redrafting the merged pattern as a new design.

Pleated Fabrics

Have you ever seen a painting worked on a three-dimensional background of long ridges with triangular cross-sections? The two sides of the ridges can be painted with quite different pictures, so that the "canvas" changes from one picture to the other as you move past it. A similar effect can produce exciting iridescent fabrics.

Someone brought an amazing thrift-store blouse to one of my classes. With vertical white and black stripes, evenly spaced, this fabric was not iridescent when laid out flat. But it had been mechanically pleated along the stripes, and the black and white shifted and rippled

This triple-weave commercial fabric consists of red, yellow, and blue layers connected at regular intervals by loom stitching. In addition, these joined layers create attractive moiré effects. The yellow center layer shows through both the blue and the red to create iridescence, but the lowest layer does not really show on the surface, as it might if the sett and beat were more open.

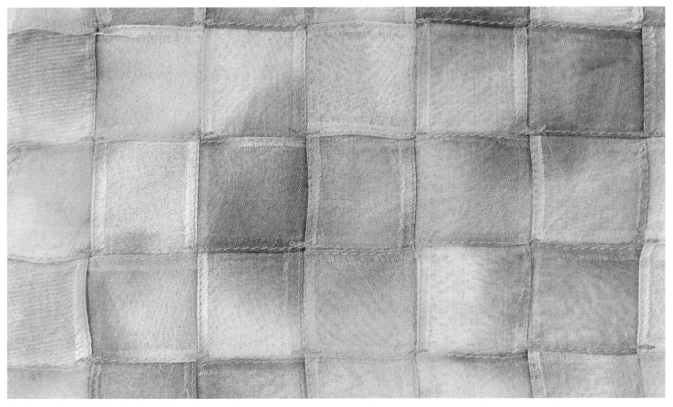

A sheer fabric, cut into wide strips and then rewoven manually as warp and weft, has potential to create interesting iridescence. This factory-made fabric is not iridescent (color changes are from variegated dyeing), but it could be inspiration for interesting experiments. It also exhibits moiré patterns.

Designed and woven by Cynthia Broughton, this sample incorporates a moiré pattern of parallel undulating lines on an iridescent background. 20/2 mercerized cotton, 24 shafts. Sample courtesy of Cynthia Broughton.

dramatically as you moved the fabric. Pleats act like the natural ridges and valleys in a woven cloth, on an exaggerated scale, creating planes of reflection.

This blouse fabric had an added enhancement, in that the pleats were not always creased at the same place on the stripes. Each pleat moved over slightly, maybe only a thread or two, and this created even more of an effect of color movement. The crease location might move gradually from the center of a black stripe, for example, to the center of a white stripe.

Trying to pleat a fabric with an iron is an exercise in futility! There are pleating machines, sold primarily for smocking or shibori, which you might want to

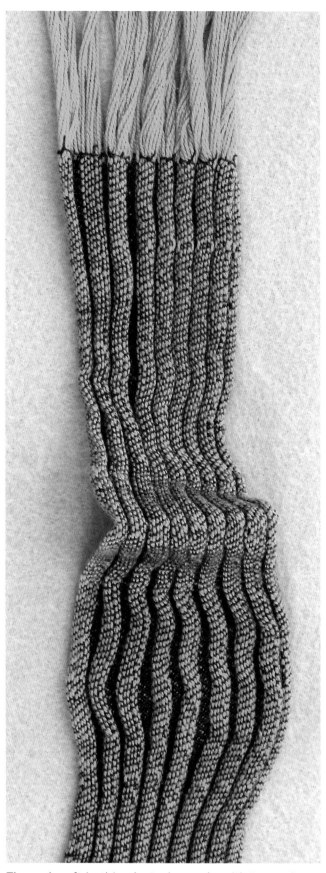

The red weft in this pleated sample with turquoise warp shows in the warp-dominant ridges and creates traditional two-color iridescence.

Although the texture is very subtle, this factory-woven blouse fabric is essentially pleated on a very fine scale. The stripes consist of four ends of black next to four ends of shiny blue, and the structure is unbalanced twill (3/1 vs. 1/3). Adjacent stripes have the opposite twill diagonals. All the color effect is in the warp.

investigate if you want to pleat a fabric mechanically. These automatically gather and crease fabric as desired. Using the structures described below, a woven fabric will often pleat by itself.

In a warp-striped woven fabric that owes its iridescence to pleating and has a weft color that blends in with the warp, all the color effect is usually in the warpwise direction (weftwise, for horizontal pleats with a "disappearing" warp). If warp and weft are contrasting colors, the ridges themselves may be iridescent in a more traditional way.

The most common structure for vertical pleats uses alternating stripes of warp-dominant (3/1) and weft-dominant (1/3) twill; 3/1 twill forms a ridge on the top face of the fabric (and a valley on the other side, where its structure is 1/3), and the 1/3 twill forms valleys on the surface and 3/1 ridges on the reverse. If the weft is considerably finer than the warp and beaten firmly, it has little influence on the structure and usually allows the natural push and pull of adjacent stripes to pleat as soon as tension is released from the warp. The warp-dominant stripes don't allow maximum packing of the weft. Wet-finishing accentuates the texture. The ridges are rounded, and a half-inch (1.3 cm) stripe width works well (if the stripes are too wide, they tend to flatten; if too narrow, the effect is muted).

Vertical stripes require eight shafts; the heavier yarn is in the warp, sett for an unbalanced twill. I prefer a 4:1 ratio in yarn sizes, with the heavier yarn four times the size of the finer yarn. I cross 5/2 cotton with 20/2 cotton, or 10/2 cotton with sewing thread. I have seen effective pleating using the same size warp and weft, but I have not had success with this. Many of these fabrics will start pleating on the loom as soon as tension is released. Wet-finishing and pulling the fabric in the warpwise direction (same direction as the ridges) will enhance the pleats.

With four shafts, you can weave horizontal pleats. In this case, the fine yarn is the warp, and the weft is heavier

My black-and-white striped fabric (below) is not iridescent when laid flat, while the colors ripple across the pleated version (at right). I also changed warp color at the center of a structural stripe, so that one side of the pleat would reflect black and the other, white. All of the color effect is in the warp; the fine weft is not obvious.

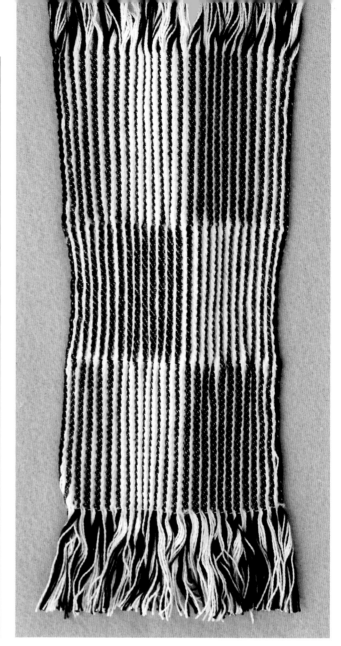

vertical pleats

horizontal pleats

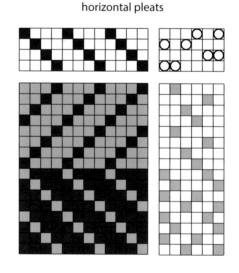

alternate treadling

Pleats can be created with 8-shaft and 4-shaft versions of unbalanced twill fabrics.

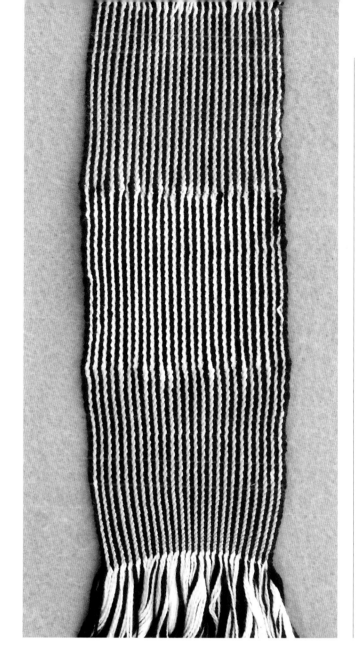

This sample at left with Lycra thread for weft was woven on the same warp as the samples on page 86, and while it's iridescent, its pleats are tighter than I'd like. As in the tale of Goldilocks and the Three Bears, this one was too much; the original (page 86 on left) was not enough; and the intermediate version (page 86, upper left) was just right!

(using the same size ratio as for vertical pleats). Alternate treadling narrow stripes of 1/3 twill and 3/1 twill. This fabric is not as practical as vertical pleats, because of limitations in the width of the fabric and the need to put the finer yarn in the warp.

If the fabric does not pleat on its own, you can weave or baste in a gathering thread, a technique also used for shibori. Another approach is to use a fine, stretchy weft yarn; this works best with a singles yarn rather than a plied yarn. Since my black-and-white pleated fabric uncharacteristically refused to pleat on its own, I wove another sample using a fine wool singles yarn with a bit of extra twist, and I stretched the weft as I closed the shed, to encourage the fabric to draw in. From sewing suppliers, you can purchase elastic thread, which can make very tight pleats, especially if you stretch it in the shed.

Although woven in plain weave and not pleated, all the color in this ribbon is in the warp, as in some pleated fabrics. The alternating red and green warps are very fine metallic ribbons, and the weft is colorless monofilament, possibly nylon. Textile analysis courtesy of Rosalie Nielson.

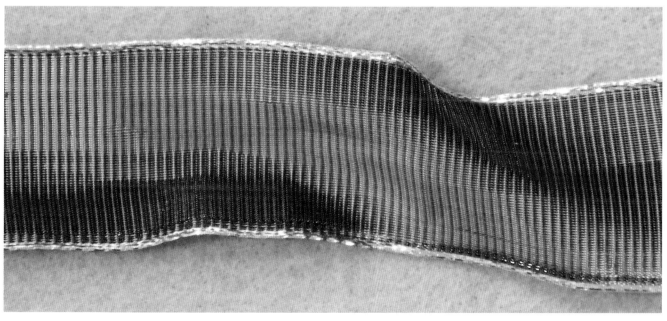

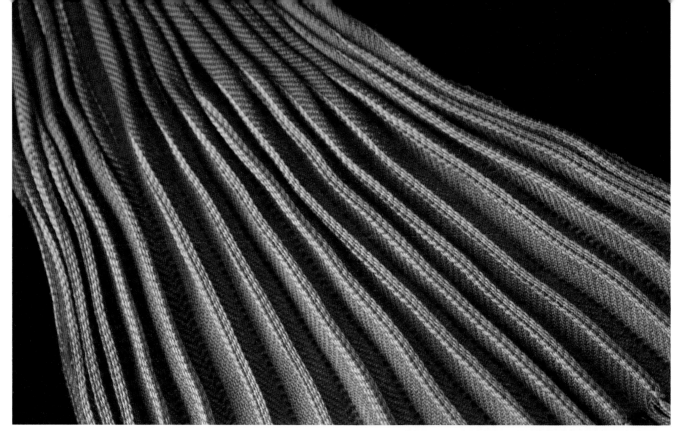

This pleated scarf by Wendy Morris ripples with orange and red-violet. A treadling change brings each color to the forefront periodically. The warp is 30/2 silk in gentian, bright magenta, orange, and rouge, at 38 e.p.i. for the crests and valleys, and 28 e.p.i. for the sides of the pleats. The weft is 60/2 silk. Photo courtesy of Wendy Morris.

Wendy Morris has devised a way of weaving pleats with sharp peaks rather than the rounded effect of alternating unbalanced twills. She uses straight twill threadings in opposite directions for the sides of the pleats and point twill for the ridges (and valleys), often with different colors for each side and just a few contrasting threads at the peaks. The folds of the pleats have a closer warp spacing.

Pile Fabrics

While pile fabrics tend not to be iridescent, there are exceptions if the ground can show through. Corduroy alternates pile ridges with valleys of the ground, and if there is enough color contrast, the effect can be similar to a pleated fabric.

Velvet is a warp-pile fabric that is not normally iridescent, yet there are numerous commercial velvets that display iridescence. A contrasting ground color can show

This commercial corduroy fabric is iridescent in black and red.

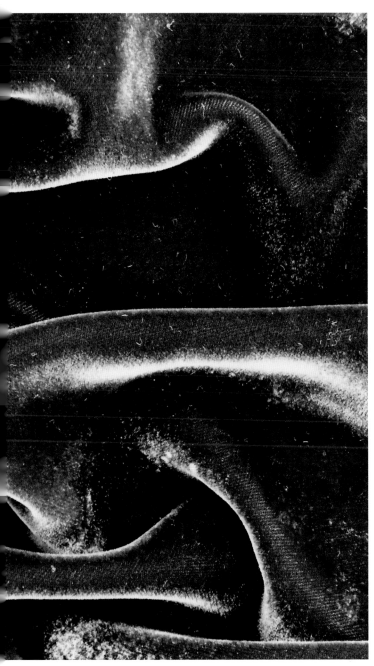

This commercial velvet is quite iridescent, with green pile and a red ground. Complementary colors are often used for this effect, and the back side often shows the iridescence better than the surface.

might be a good candidate for iridescence. During the mid-1800s, velvet with two pile colors was popular. This *chameleon* velvet was iridescent.

Although I haven't seen iridescence in velveteen, a weft-pile fabric similar to velvet, there may be some iridescent velveteens. These fabrics are usually woven with less expensive and less lustrous threads, so they have a more matte appearance.

An increasing number of handweavers are weaving velvet these days. Handwoven velvet is usually heavier than factory-woven velvet and less likely to show two-color iridescence. Fine-grouped pile warps in handwoven velvet interlace more visibly with the ground and show on the back side as well as in voided areas, so any color contrast between the pile and ground cloth produces a blended effect. In commercial iridescent velvet, the pile tends to be shorter, finer, and much less visible in the ground cloth, which is also finer. The intersections of pile and ground are only evident on close inspection, although there is enough color from the pile on the back side so that the colors can shift. The iridescence is usually more obvious on the back side and is more subtle on the front.

Satin/Sateen

The same woman who brought the pleated blouse to class brought a second amazing thrift-store blouse as well. This one was primarily yellow-green, with mysterious flashes of lustrous blue-violet as you moved it. An analysis in class, with the help of a good magnifier, revealed that the structure was satin.

Satin is a warp-faced fabric that would not normally be iridescent. A twill weave, satin has long warp floats tied down by the weft at intervals; the twill structure is not visible on the lustrous surface because the closely spaced warps nest together. The reverse side shows only the weft. In this unusual blouse fabric, the yellow-green weft was much heavier than the blue-violet warp, and where it tied down the warp floats, it pushed the warps aside enough to show through. The iridescence was perfect for its intended use as dance costume—I have since found similar blouses, always in thrift stores and probably dating from the disco era of the 1970s! Occasionally I've found iridescent satin yardage in fabric stores, such as the black-and-white satin shown in the top photo on page 37.

Warp-faced satin is normally woven with Z-twist warp and weft and Z twill to keep the warp twill line from being obvious. Iridescent satin is woven the same, and it is the thread-size difference that is most responsible for

through a fine velvet pile in some cases. Voided velvet (where pile is deliberately not woven in certain areas), devoré (where chemical treatment removes some pile), and embossed velvet, which has a pattern pressed into the pile, can allow a contrasting ground to show through.

Velvet varies considerably in the density of its pile. *Chiffon* velvet, sometimes called *transparent* velvet, has a very lightweight pile on a sheer silk or rayon base and

The iridescence in this factory-woven satin fabric is dramatic!

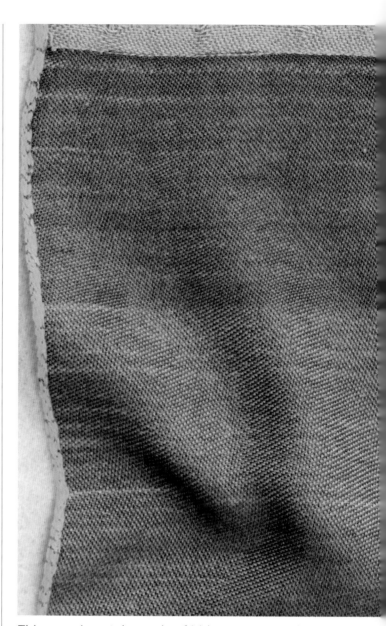

This experimental sample of iridescent sateen has a 20/2 mercerized cotton warp (turquoise) at 80 e.p.i. and a weft of shiny pink rayon sewing thread, which is considerably finer. A relatively gentle beat helped the warp show through, with about 64 picks per inch.

the effect. The Z-twist yarns and Z twill also tend to make the weft twill more prominent.

Sateen is the weft-faced version of satin, with the long floats in the weft. Weaving iridescent sateen is much easier than weaving satin because you put the very fine thread in the weft and use a heavier warp. When you cross yarns of distinctly different sizes this way, it's important to use a much closer sett than normal. Average the plain weave setts of the two yarns.

Woven without regard to the effect of yarn twist or twill direction, my sateen samples used S-ply warp, Z-ply weft, and Z twill. This does tend to make the twill structure more distinct.

Capturing the Natural Spectrum

Some textiles have been designed to mimic the multicolored effects of certain natural iridescent substances , such as oil slicks or soap bubbles. Perhaps this takes more skill than crossing colors the "easy" way, and it seems to be a legitimate approach. Some of these fabrics shift colors as the angle of view changes; some are more static, as are quite a few examples of natural iridescence.

Oil Spill, an award-winning shawl by Agnes Hauptli, glows with iridescent color combinations. The warp is 10/2 Tencel in red, blue, and green; the weft is 200/2 black silk (doubled). The sett is 36 e.p.i., and the threading has three interleaved design lines on 22 shafts. Photo courtesy of Agnes Hauptli.

Susan Wilson wove this scarf with 20/2 silk in classic 4-shaft crackle. The striped warp has 11 colors, which are also rotated through the ground and pattern wefts. Photo courtesy of Susan Wilson.

This factory-made fabric shines with multiple colors from its very reflective surface.

One of the easiest ways to get a multicolored effect is to weave with Mylar and similar yarns that reflect a full spectrum of colors. There are many examples of commercial fabrics using these materials, and it doesn't require a contrasting base color to produce a glitzy fabric with a lot of sparkle that changes constantly as you move it.

Some fabrics in double weave, using multiple colors, incorporate areas of traditional (two-color) iridescence while giving the overall effect of natural multicolored iridescence.

Polychrome crackle and summer-and-winter can mimic the spectrum in multiple colors.

Barbara Setsu Pickett has experimented with the multicolored effect of natural iridescence in the pile of her exquisite handwoven velvet. In the first set of samples shown on pages 94–95, the pile is composed of multiple fine threads in many colors, with subtle color changes across the pile warp. Each pile unit consists of four strands of 50/3 cotton and four strands of cotton sewing thread, and there are 30 units across the width.

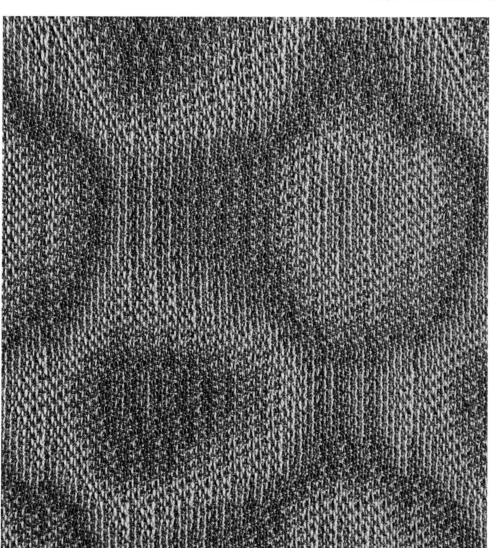

Marian Stubenitsky wove this double twill fabric with the colors and patterns of an oil slick. She used 16 shafts, four colors in the warp, and two additional weft colors. Photo by Joke van den Broek, courtesy of Marian Stubenitsky.

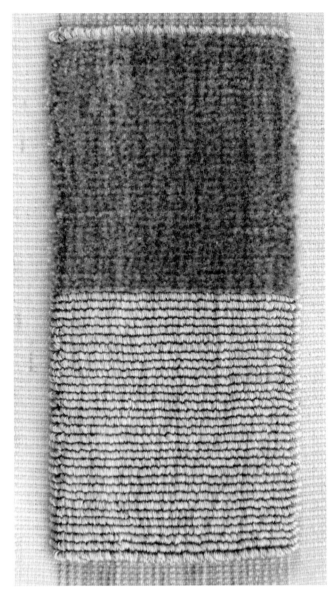

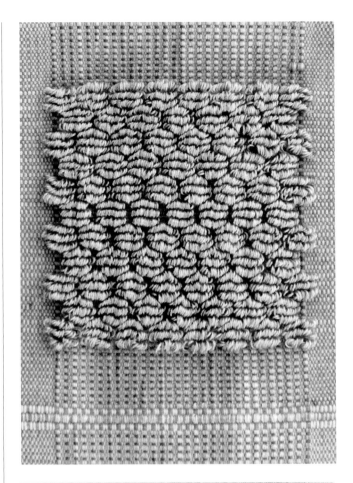

In these velvet samples by Barbara Setsu Pickett, the intricate color changes across the warp are especially evident in the uncut pile (below), which reflects light better than the cut pile (above).

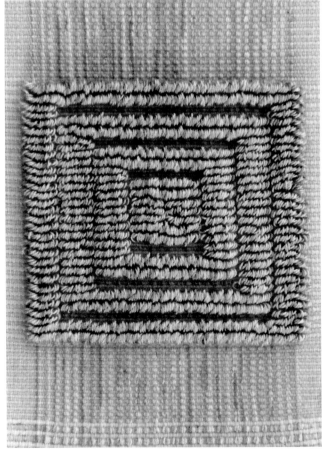

On the same warp, Barbara has also sampled voided velvet, leaving the pile unwoven in certain areas. Note how the pile warps are visible where interwoven with the background.

This sample on the same warp alternates horizontal rows of cut pile with rows of uncut pile. The uncut pile reflects the light best and is especially prominent when the fabric is flexed.

In these samples with more saturated pile colors, there are fewer threads in the pile units, so the background shows more readily in the voided sample (top). All the pile units contain one thread each of the same three colors, dark gold and coral in 20/2 mercerized cotton, plus turquoise in 50/3 cotton. In the solid uncut pile (bottom), changing colors appear to ripple across when the fabric is flexed.

Focus on Fashion

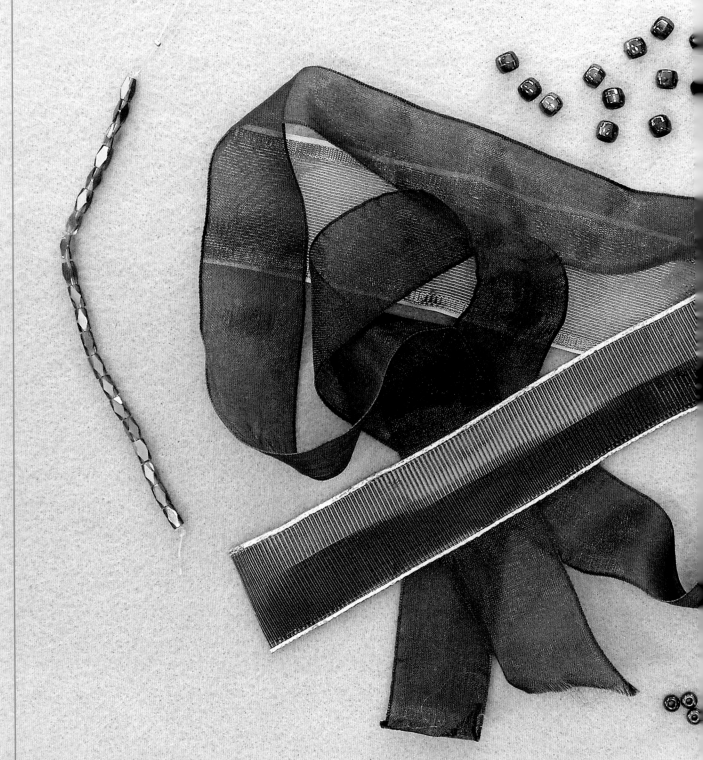

Iridescence has always been especially desirable in clothing fabrics, particularly fine cloth for special occasions. Ideal for the spotlights of a fashion show runway, these garments are guaranteed to attract attention! In clothing and fabric stores, you are most likely to find iridescent fabrics in sections devoted to party, dance, and formal wear.

While you may be just as enchanted with a table runner that appears to change color, I encourage you to design iridescent fabrics to wear. A scarf is a wonderful and relatively quick way of sampling different yarns, colors, and structures. An iridescent scarf will bring you many compliments and will likely sell quickly if you are marketing your handwoven accessories.

Do consider the color choices; just because something is iridescent does not mean everyone will like it. The effects can be dramatic or subtle; something in appropriate tints may be ideal for everyday wear, and saturated colors in high-luster yarns may be more suitable for an evening out. Many people will be looking for colors that suit their personal palettes, based on skin tone, so analogous colors may be just right for them. Few of us look wonderful wearing complementary colors, except for certain people with cool complexions who can wear black and saturated colors with flair.

Choosing a Pattern

Some pattern features are especially good at showing off iridescent fabrics. Because we see the color shift better when a fabric is crumpled, patterns with pleats, gathers, shirring, smocking, puckers, and ruffles can accentuate the color changes.

Sewing with Handwoven Fabric

There are numerous sources of information about sewing with handwoven fabric, written by people much more adept than I am, and I recommend you refer to them. However, here are some guidelines to keep in mind when sewing any handwoven clothing fabric, with some specific recommendations for iridescent fabric.

Handwoven fabrics are often heavier than commercial fabrics. I've found that adding a lining may make the garment too heavy and reduce its finished size because of the extra bulk, so I choose blouse patterns (for example) that are not intended to be lined. Many handweavers are very reluctant to cut into their fabric, but it becomes easier the more you do it. Because handwoven fabric usually lacks sizing, raw edges must be secured quickly when the fabric comes off the loom and as you cut into it.

Factory-woven fabric comes in standard widths, most often 36 inches, 44 to 45 inches, and 60 inches. Commercial sewing patterns tell you what lengths to purchase depending on body size and the available width of a bolt of fabric. Few handweavers produce anything close to those standard widths, and even when it's possible, in most cases it is far more efficient and faster to weave a longer length of a narrower fabric rather than to attempt to duplicate industry standards. Your loom dictates the maximum width you can produce, so pattern sections that are too wide for your equipment are impractical

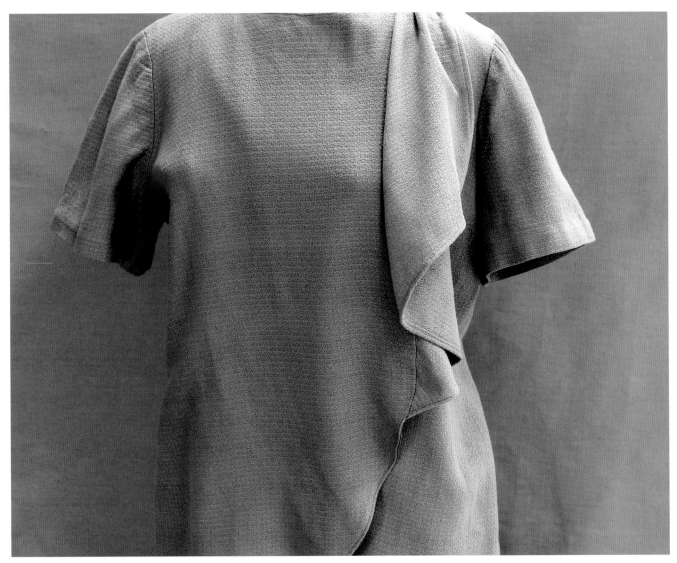

This blouse has a drape at the front that shows off its iridescence. Simplicity pattern #7427, 1996.

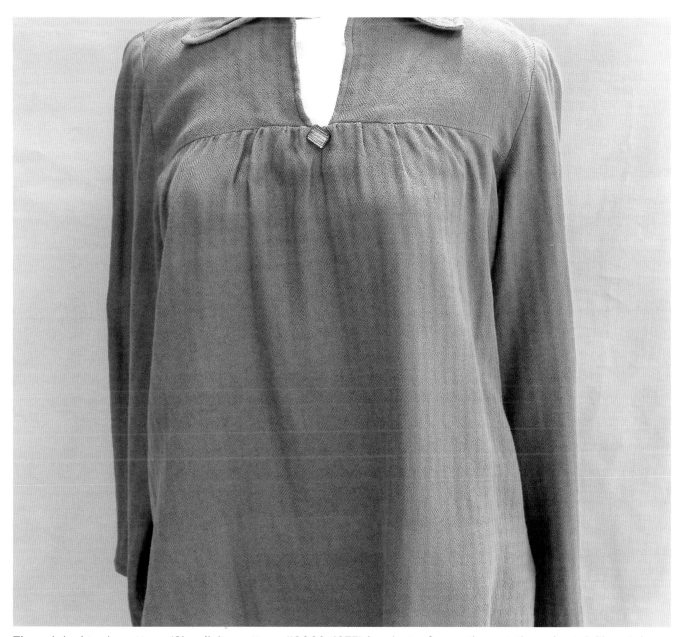

The original tunic pattern (Simplicity pattern #8060, 1977) has just a few gathers at the yoke. I deliberately cut the lower front section wider than the pattern called for so I could add more gathering.

unless you can cut them narrower and seam them. In order to finish a particular width, handwoven clothing fabric must almost always be woven considerably wider to make up for draw-in and shrinkage.

Using a temple when weaving is advantageous, especially for fine yarns and fabrics wider than scarves. A temple can also be a nuisance when it interferes with your view of the fabric at and near the fell, and it needs to be moved frequently. Some weavers always use them; some avoid them unless absolutely necessary. Even with a temple, there will be some draw-in and shrinkage in width because, except in rep weaves, our wefts travel over and

under warps, not straight across a row, and there is always some take-up. Remember, it's this three-dimensionality of our cloth that enhances its iridescence by reflecting the light.

Full-width sampling is essential when you are working with any yarn you are not well familiar with. Keeping good notes as you weave helps you plan similar projects with confidence. Also, always plan to weave a fabric wider and longer than you think you'll need, especially if you'll need to match structural blocks or other patterns at seams. It's better to end up with extra fabric than to run short because of undetected treadling errors, for example.

I call this jacket "Copper Ore," because the red and yellow warps discussed on page 102 blend to look like copper, and the blue and green wefts are like the beautiful ores of copper. Adapted from McCall's pattern #4259, 1974.

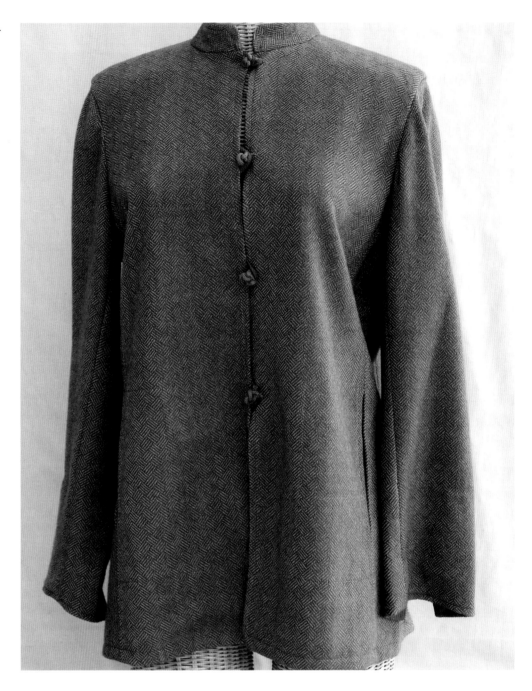

There are some patterns available designed by weavers for handwoven fabrics, but in most cases I prefer to use commercial patterns. I've assembled an extensive library of old patterns that fit me and appeal to me (old patterns, sometimes unused, are often available at thrift stores, although used patterns may be missing crucial pieces). Just because you can only weave 24 inches wide does not mean you can't adapt your fabric for many patterns. I rarely follow the suggested pattern layout because it's adapted for wider fabrics than I produce. Instead, I lay out the pattern on the floor or a table to find the most practical length and width required before I put a warp on the loom.

Use the widest pattern piece (usually the back, for a blouse, vest, or jacket) to determine the maximum width you must weave, adding extra for draw-in and shrinkage. If you cannot weave a fabric that wide, either choose a more accommodating pattern or seam the back. This requires careful matching of fabric design, and you must add a seam allowance for each half of the back section in order to create a center seam.

Commercial fabrics on bolts are usually folded, and some pattern pieces are designed to be placed on the fold (the back, for example). Also, with two layers of fabric, items such as sleeves are meant to be cut as a pair, and they will automatically be the reverse of each other. This will not be the case with your handwoven fabric, so you will have to remember to flip the pattern (front to back) for cutting the second piece.

If you wish, you can copy pattern pieces onto large pieces of paper so you are sure that all are in the orientation you want them, and that you haven't neglected to cut pieces that need to be cut twice. "End rolls" of blank newsprint are often available from newspaper companies at little cost, and they work well for copying pattern sections. Weavers who plan to reuse patterns may choose to make them more permanent by copying onto nonfusible interfacing.

If I know I will be cutting my fabric rather than fringing it, I start and end the fabric on the loom by overcasting the edge by hand with half-inch (1.3 cm) stitches. This doesn't require counting warps or being precise about which weft row you stitch through; it's just to stabilize the ends temporarily until you have time to secure them off the loom.

Keep track of your fabric width and length on the loom as well as in its relaxed state as soon as it comes off the loom, and keep these records for future reference. Before you wash the fabric, make any needed corrections to unwanted floats or other errors, using a blunt-tipped tapestry needle that is not too bulky (the large plastic ones are not good for this purpose). A lighted magnifying lamp makes this easier.

Before wet-finishing your fabric, hem under the raw edges. Wash, dry, and press your fabric appropriately for the fiber content; for cotton and rayon, I normally machine launder my fabric, at least the first time. Lay out each pattern piece carefully, maintaining the desired orientation. With iridescence created by crossing two colors at right angles, pieces cut perpendicular to others will tend to show a different color when viewed from the same angle. This can be attractive for side panels and small pieces such as pockets and collars. Don't lay out your pieces in different orientations unless you plan this

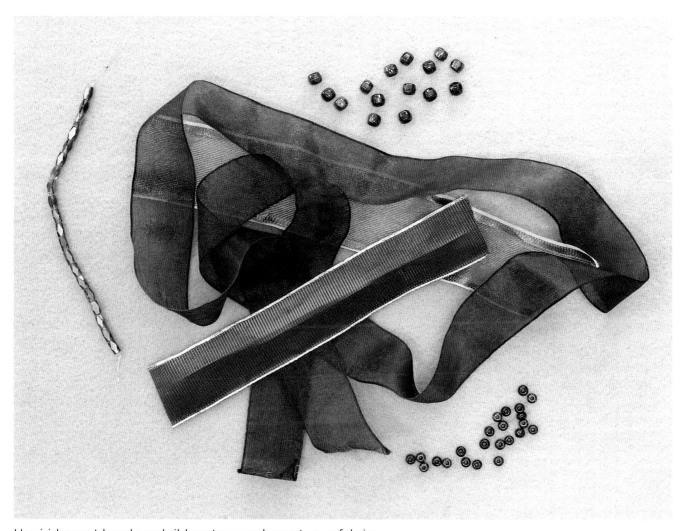

Use iridescent beads and ribbon to complement your fabrics.

Wear iridescent jewelry to match your fabrics: earrings (these are saganishiki by Jan Paul, a Japanese technique using gold paper woven with silk); opal and dichroic glass pendants; a dichroic glass button worn as a pin; and an abalone shell brooch.

effect deliberately. With a four-color fabric, cutting certain pieces with pattern pieces flipped top to bottom can accentuate a second weft color for visual contrast.

Once you are certain you've laid out the pattern pieces efficiently and correctly and have pinned them securely to the fabric, cut fabric sections one at a time. Mark the right side with a safety pin away from seam lines and immediately secure the cut edges with serging or a zig-zag stitch. Keep the safety pins in place during assembly. Rather than using a serger to join sections, I prefer conventional seams.

While making a jacket from the four-colored fabric shown on page 51, sample on left, I faced several challenges. The first was the width of the fabric. In order to weave at 48 e.p.i., I had to double-sley the only 24-dent reed I had available at its maximum width of 21½

inches (54.6 cm). Because I was using my adaptation of the French basketweave technique with alternating warp colors, I could not use a wider reed with different denting. The total take-up and shrinkage of the finished fabric was 21 percent in width and 10.5 percent in length, so the fabric ended up only 17 inches (43.2 cm) wide.

The jacket pattern I found had separate side panels, and I cut those to feature a different weft color from the main jacket pieces by flipping the panel pieces so they were oriented toward the opposite end of the yardage from the fronts, back, and sleeves. Since the back pattern was too wide for the fabric, I cut sections half the intended width, adding a seam allowance to each, then seamed the back at the center, matching the woven pattern as carefully as possible.

Caring for Your Iridescent Fabrics

I normally wash and dry cotton fabrics by machine, at least to finish the fabric before sewing it. The first iridescent blouse I made, which I wear frequently, has been washed and dried numerous times in my washer and dryer with regular laundry detergent, fading it and dulling the luster. Consequently, I now hand wash my special creations with shampoo or another mild cleanser, spin them in the washer, press while damp, then put them on a drying rack to dry. Some fading may be inevitable, but the gentler laundering helps preserve the luster.

According to some sources, Tencel benefits from repeated machine washing and thorough machine drying. It has a tendency to produce fine pills that result in a suede-like texture and a wonderful hand. Some luster may be lost in the process, however, so you need to experiment and finish the fabric appropriately in order to achieve your desired results.

Open-weave fabrics such as some double weaves and leno should be hand washed to minimize distortion. Most silk can be machine washed on gentle cycle without alkaline detergent; remove before the spin cycle is complete to avoid permanent creases. It sometimes ends up a bit stiff; slapping the dry fabric against a hard surface makes it more supple. Linen starts stiff and softens the more it is washed, and it will stand up to machine washing well as long as ends are securely hemmed under. Do not let wrinkles set; give the fabric a hard press before it is dry. Like silk, linen can benefit from being slapped against a hard surface to reduce its stiffness.

Fringe needs to be twisted or secured before machine washing, in particular. Some yarns such as Tencel are especially prone to raveling if unsecured during laundering. Many of my workshop samples have unfinished fringe to show the component colors, but twisting the fringe will make it last longer.

Accessories for Your Iridescent Fashions

There are many exciting buttons, beads, and jewelry options suitable for your handwoven clothing, and many of them are themselves iridescent. You might choose a single expensive button that complements your fabric and the woven design, or add iridescent beads to fringe in appropriate colors. I'm particularly fond of dichroic glass buttons, which I sometimes use as pins or pendants, and Czech glass beads. Abalone shell beads and other accessories are often available in hobby stores, and opal jewelry is a nice match for certain fabrics.

Options for Spinners, Dyers, and Knitters

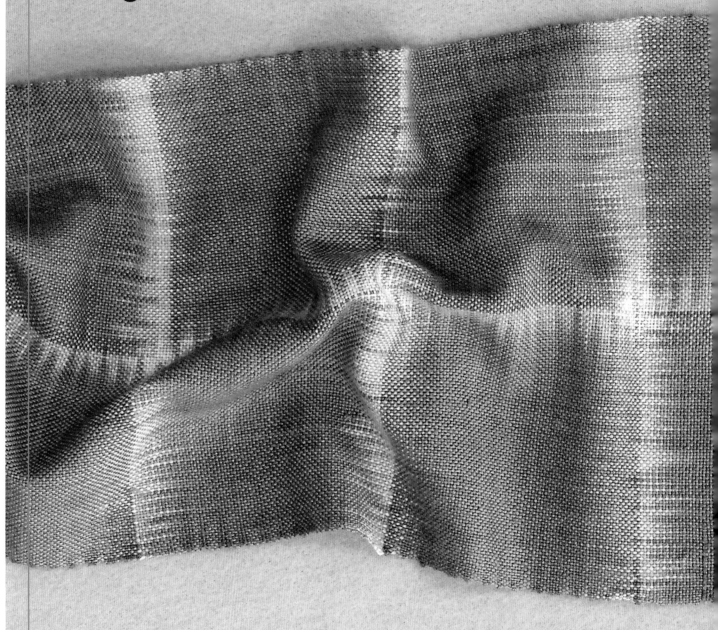

CHAPTER NINE

Spinning for Iridescence

If you are a spinner, you can control fiber content, spinning method, size, twist, texture, and color. Some options are not available currently in factory-spun yarns, so if you want a Z-plied yarn that you can't find in a store, for example, you can spin your own. You can control the amount and direction of twist in both a singles and a plied yarn.

Choosing lustrous fibers with relatively long staple length can help your handspun yarns glow. If you wish to work with animal fiber, a long and lustrous staple is a good choice for iridescence, and a worsted-spun yarn will be smoother with more luster than a woolen-spun yarn. Many textured yarns interfere with light reflection, although "beads" of a fiber such as rayon will catch the light well. The more plies you put into a yarn, the more the twist will interfere with reflection.

Spinners can also incorporate iridescent fibers such as Angelina, polyester fiber that comes in many colorways and can add a sparkle to the yarn even in small amounts. These fibers reflect a rainbow of colors, accenting particular base colors while giving the effect of natural multicolored iridescence.

Using solid-colored fiber in two or more colors, you can achieve the effect of a space-dyed yarn by controlling the length and sequence of color repeats, for extra color excitement in fabric. (Yarn with relatively short color segments is easiest to design with.) You can add iridescent beads or sequins during plying.

Take advantage of some lustrous fibers such as ramie, soy silk, Ingeo (corn fiber) and SeaCell (fiber from seaweed), which are more readily available to spinners than they are in commercial yarns. Rayon, polyester, and other synthetics are sometimes available as unspun fiber. While many of the fibers are natural or white, some are available dyed, and all can be custom dyed. With carding or combing, you can create unusual blends that are not available either in prepared fiber or as commercial yarns. You can also ply commercial yarns with handspun, or ply different fibers or colors together.

Dye Your Own Color-Play Yarns

Dyers can work with commercial as well as handspun yarns. Dyed 20/2 pearl cotton is currently available only in a limited color range, and 20/2 Tencel is only available in white or as custom-dyed yarn. You can dye these commercial natural or white yarns any colors you wish. Unusual sizes are sometimes available in undyed yarn, providing exciting options you can dye for weaving.

I have seen velvet with pile painted blue and the opposite side, the ground, dyed orange. This produced iridescence in a factory fabric that started as pure white.

Shibori and woven shibori can give iridescent effects in pleated cloth. Hand-painted warps (and/or wefts) can create a kaleidoscope of shifting colors throughout a fabric. You can design your own space-dyed yarns for crossing with each other or with solid colors. Specific, predictable color repeats can be easier to control in the weaving than spot-dyeing. Use a limited color range of analogous colors in each yarn, distinct color families, and relatively short color segments for best results.

In my desire to create shifting blocks side by side that have the same two colors in opposite orientations, the best result I found for a lightweight, drapable fabric required dyeing warp and weft in specific color repeats.

This man-made (Angelina Mylar) fiber reflects multiple colors.

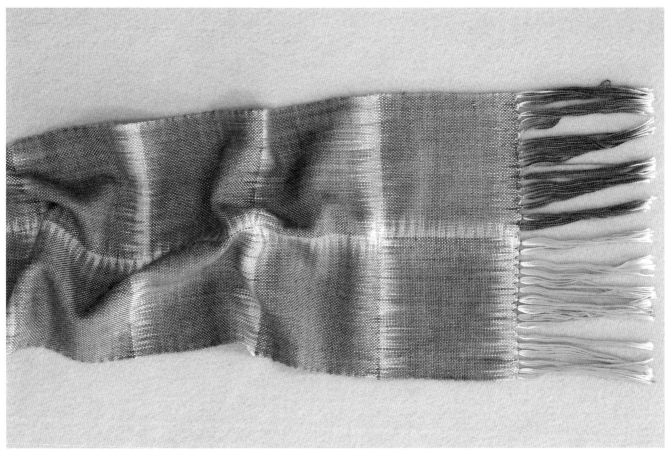

20/2 silk scarf in plain weave at 24 e.p.i.; yarn and dyeing courtesy of J. Elff, RedFish DyeWorks.

The resulting fabric required precise measurement during dyeing and careful alignment on the loom. This created a warp- and weft-ikat effect by aligning one warp color with the second weft color, and vice versa. The adjacent blocks shift from blue to pink as the fabric moves.

The warp yarn was carefully dyed with a 6-inch (15.2 cm) color repeat alternating 3-inch (7.6 cm) sections of pink and blue, and was aligned on the loom to create blocks of alternating colors, both side by side and vertically. The weft required a 12-inch (30.5 cm) color repeat, 6 inches (15.2 cm) of pink alternating with 6 inches of blue, because the weft doubles back on itself as you weave. The weft was carefully aligned in the shed so that pink weft wove on the blue warp blocks and blue weft on the pink warp sections. Resists were tied tightly to prevent color mixing between blue and pink, showing as undyed areas of white between the colors. Letting the colors blend would be another option that would add a purple mix to the overall effect.

My original plan to have three stripes of warp blocks alternating horizontally and vertically would require even more planning and two different wefts with 15-inch (38.1 cm) repeats. One would be dyed with 6 inches (15.2 cm) of blue, 3 inches (7.6 cm) of pink, and 6 inches (15.2 cm) of blue, repeated. The other would be 6 pink, 3 blue, and 6 pink. Only the colors at the sides double back on themselves.

Iridescent Knitted Fabrics

Can a knitted fabric be iridescent? One would not normally expect knitting to exhibit iridescence because its looped structure does not cross colored threads in the same manner as in weaving. Yet there are several ways to make a knitted fabric iridescent. The striped and pleated blouse mentioned earlier was a knitted fabric.

I have several samples of three-colored iridescent fabrics (sheer commercial knits) with a solid background, printed with lustrous material in various patterns . . . stars, leopard spots, spider webs, and the like . . . in more than one color. The effect is quite striking; however this technology isn't generally available to knitters.

This sheer knit fabric is printed with iridescent patterns.

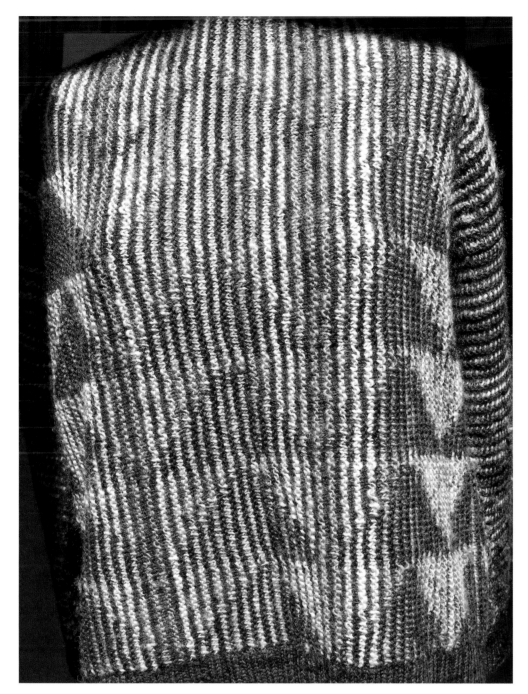

This sweater, designed and knit by Susan Wilson, shows triangular patterns as the result of shadow knitting. The same patterns are present throughout, although they are less obvious seen from certain angles and depending on the lighting.

There is an effect in knitted fabric, popularized as "shadow knitting" by Vivian Høxbro in her 2004 book of the same name. Likely originally a Japanese technique, this method uses stitch variations (knit/stockinette versus purl/garter stitch) and dark and light color alternations to produce patterns that appear and disappear at certain angles (and show color variations).

In shadow knitting, two rows of one color alternate with two rows of the other, worked from the wrong side. Purl stitches create ridges on the right side, knit stitches appear as valleys, and the stitches change to give the effect of patterns that become more distinct at certain angles. Because these fabrics always contain more than one color, I do consider this to be an example of iridescence, similar in structure and effect to striped and pleated woven fabrics.

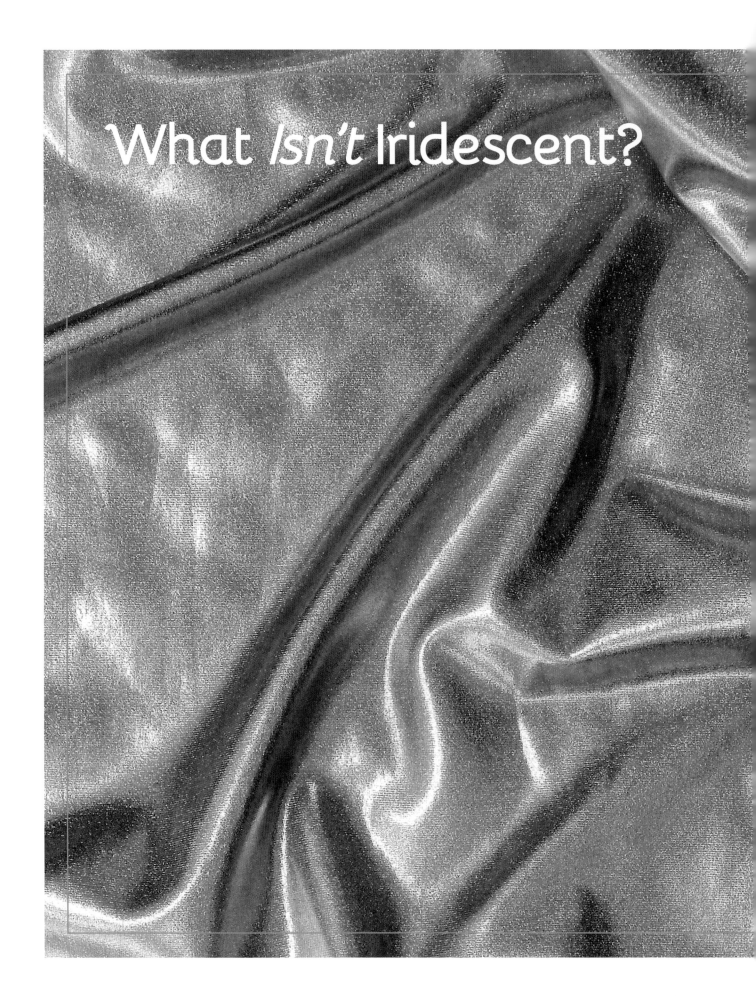

What *Isn't* Iridescent?

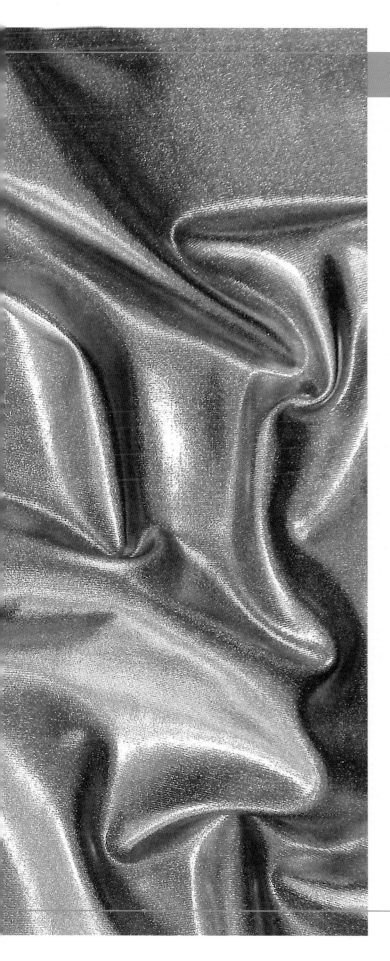

CHAPTER TEN

After many years of weaving iridescent cloth, I almost have trouble weaving anything that isn't when I'm working with more than one color. Yet not everything that's colorful and lustrous is iridescent. Over the years, people have given me samples of commercial fabrics as examples of iridescence . . . and some of them are not. I've also collected a number of examples that mimic iridescence but contain only one color.

While pleats, puckers, folds, and crinkles often enhance the iridescence of a fabric, they don't work if the fabric is a solid color. Any solid-colored fabric, when crumpled, will show apparent dark and light color variations solely from the effects of shadows and reflection.

Colorful, yes, but these printed colors don't shift. This might be considered an example of capturing the multicolored effect of natural iridescence.

The extreme luster of this printed surface gives the illusion of iridescence at first glance, but it's all one color, and you see only light and shadow. Where the fabric is reflecting all colors, it looks white in the photograph.

Just because a fabric has metallic threads doesn't make it iridescent. There is no color shifting in this one with metallic components that give the effect of gold and silver.

An iridescent fabric cannot consist of just one color. It must contain at least two colors or a thread that reflects more than one color.

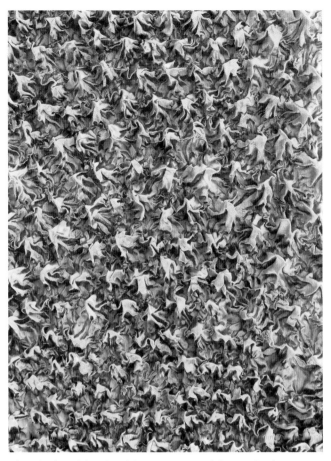

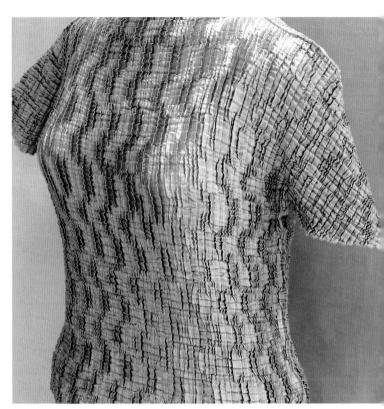

The darker blue in this "popcorn" blouse is the result of shadows, not iridescence. The fabric is all the same color.

This interesting blouse fabric is pleated in different directions to produce patterns that change with the angle of view and look light and dark, but there is no real shift in color. The fabric is all the same color, and the darker areas are shadows.

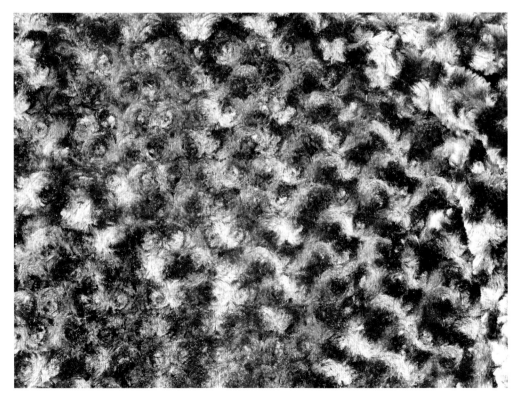

This faux fur fabric is crushed in places and appears to be two colors, but that is an illusion, and all the color variation is the result of light and shadow.

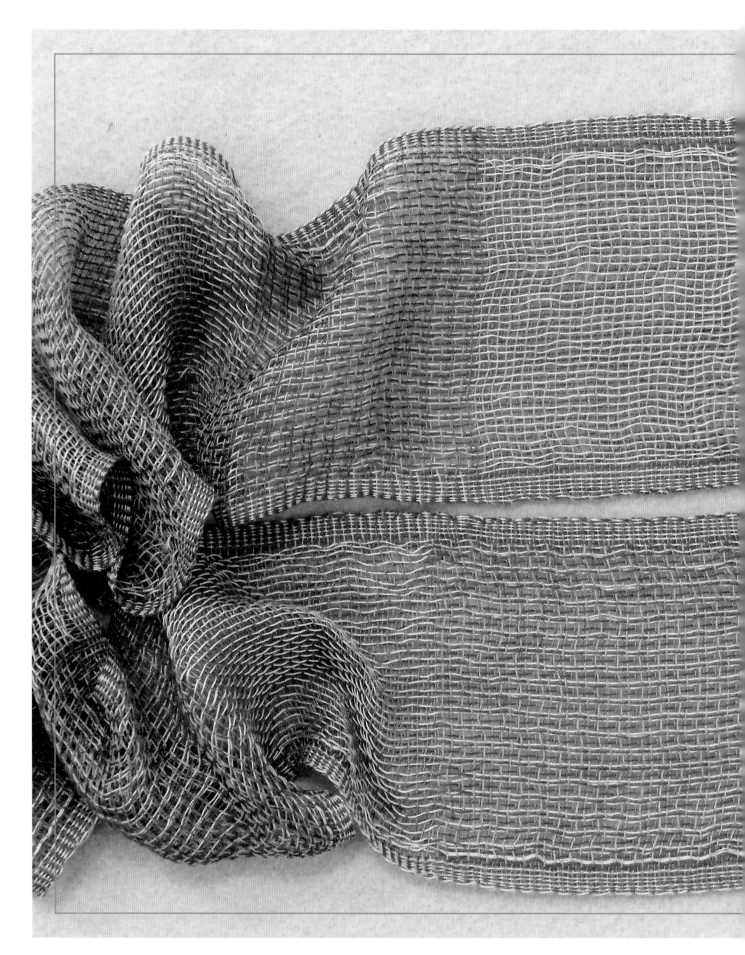

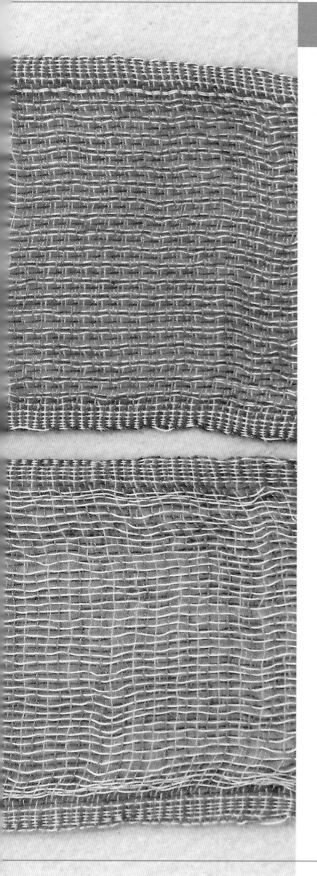

CHAPTER ELEVEN

Projects

These projects require from four to eight shafts and will give you useful color samples, as well as the opportunity to try some special techniques for creating iridescent fabrics suitable for household goods, clothing, and wearable accessories. *Please review the written instructions before preparing your warps.* The written instructions may indicate, better than the actual drafts, changes in setts, colors, and beat within a project. In some cases, I recommend weaving a certain number of inches before changing the treadling, rather than a specific number of picks, because your beat can vary. You can figure out specific numbers for treadling repeats as you weave.

The yardages given should be more than adequate for the intended uses and can be adapted to different sizes and loom widths as needed. The amount of fabric you can weave depends largely on your preferred warping method, equipment, and habits. Reeds mentioned in the instructions are American-style, not metric, e.g. 12-dent means 12 dents per inch.

If I plan to fringe a piece, I hemstitch instead of tying overhand knots, using a tail of weft about three times the width of the warp. If I know I will be hemming the ends (including for yardage I will be cutting for sewing), I use a tail of weft about one-and-a-half times the width of the warp and quickly overcast the edge at the start and finish. This secures the ends temporarily until I can serge or zigzag them and hem them under before wet-finishing. There is no need to count threads, and my stitches zigzag in and out of the fabric at about half-inch intervals. The stitching will not show when hemmed under.

Wet-finishing is an important part of the process for almost all fabrics. Choose a method appropriate to the fiber and fabric—by hand or machine—and use a mild cleanser. Fringe must be secured, preferably twisted, before wet-finishing.

Spectrum Napkins

This project uses 12 colors of mercerized (pearl) cotton and will be a handy reference for what happens when you cross the colors. All blocks except the solids where the warp and weft are the same color show some degree of iridescence, and the twill floats enhance the effect. Narrow stripes of black separate the color blocks in both warp and weft and make them appear more brilliant.

To counteract the tendency of the selvedge blocks to draw in, I threaded them slightly wider than the 10 center blocks. I also wove the same colors (blue and blue-violet) longer, so that they'd match the size of the center blocks when hemmed.

Wind the warp in the color order shown on page 117, starting and ending with 52 ends of blue and blue-violet. The 10 center colors are 46 ends wide, with 2 ends of black between each color block.

Weave colors in the same order, starting with 2¼ inches (5.7 cm) of blue. Weave two picks of black, 1½ inches (3.8 cm) of blue-green, and continue with 1½-inch (3.8 cm) blocks separated by 2 picks of black. Weave the final block (blue-violet) 2¼ inches (5.7 cm). Separate the end of one napkin and the start of the next with two picks of a contrasting color to use as a cutting line during finishing.

Off the loom, make any needed corrections. Serge or zigzag the ends of the fabric, fold under ¼ inch (0.6 cm) twice, and stitch. Machine wash the fabric in warm water with a little detergent or mild soap, and machine dry warm until slightly damp. Press the fabric and hang to finish drying. Cut napkins apart and serge or zigzag the cut edges. Press under ¼ inch (0.6 cm) twice, and stitch.

PROJECT DETAILS

Set of 4 or 5 napkins (depending on loom waste)

Pattern/Structure: 2/2 twill, 4 shafts

Warp width: 19½ in. (49.5 cm) (586 ends) + floating selvedges (optional, to match the edge colors). Floating selvedges are not necessary if, for the first pick, shafts 1 and 2 are raised while you throw the shuttle toward the selvedge threaded on shaft 1.

Warp length: 3½ yd. (3.2 m)

Sett: 30 e.p.i.: 3/dent in a 10-dent reed, 2-3 in a 12-dent reed, 2/dent in a 15-dent reed

Picks per inch (2.5 cm): approx. 28. A firm beat (without using a temple) makes a twill diagonal slightly steeper than 45 degrees. When the tension is released and the fabric is washed, it relaxes to the proper twill angle.

Warp and weft: 10/2 pearl cotton at 4,200 yd. (3,840 m)/lb., from UKI/Supreme Corporation, in the same colors. The color numbers and names shown are the company's, and some retailers use their own systems. Total amounts:

Blue:	#125 Pacific Blue, 1.5 oz. (42.5 g)
Blue-green:	#135 Jade Green, 1.2 oz. (34.0 g)
Green:	#13 Sapphire, 1.2 oz. (34.0 g)
Yellow-green:	#50 Avocado, 1.2 oz. (34.0 g)
Yellow:	#113 Yellow, 1.2 oz. (34.0 g)
Yellow-orange:	#111 Dark Gold, 1.2 oz. (34.0 g)
Orange:	#11 Tangerine, 1.2 oz. (34.0 g)
Red-orange:	#149 Burnt Orange, 1.2 oz. (34.0 g)
Red:	#12 Red, 1.2 oz. (34.0 g)
Red-violet:	#102 Magenta, 1.2 oz. (34.0 g)
Violet:	#27 Purple, 1.2 oz. (34.0 g)
Blue-violet:	#93 Lavender, 1.5 oz. (42.5 g)
Black:	#116 Black, 0.6 oz. (17.0 g)

Take-up: 8% width, 4.5% length

Total shrinkage: 13% width, 7% length

Finished napkins (hemmed): 17¼ in. x 17½ in. (43.8 cm x 44.5 cm)

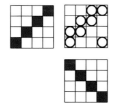

An alternate palette of lighter colors forms a second 12-color spectrum, using similar yarns and amounts. I separated the color blocks with gray instead of black. The UKI/Supreme Corporation colors I used were:

Blue:	#95 Mineral
Blue-green:	#60 Duck
Green:	#57 Willow Green
Yellow-green:	#152 Pistachio
Yellow:	#40 Light Yellow
Yellow-orange:	#10 Gold
Orange:	#67 Light Orange
Red-orange:	#107 Melon
Red:	#88 Wisteria
Red-violet:	#56 Dark Fuchsia
Violet:	#81 Grotto
Blue-violet:	#146 Periwinkle
Gray:	#141 Silver

Double-Weave Scarf

This light and airy scarf weighs only about an ounce. Four colors interact in six different combinations, and each set of six is woven three times; additional options are possible, such as exchanging warp colors with each pick. This scarf is hemmed for extra stability, and because the warp is too sparse for attractive fringe.

The 6-shaft version has single layers of plain weave at the selvedges, which help space and stabilize the wefts in the open-weave center. If you have only four shafts, you can weave a similar scarf; although it will not have single-layered edges, the closer sett at the sides will still help stabilize the open weave.

This scarf is quick to warp but slower to weave because of the need to maintain the open effect while beating. It's not designed for fancy knotting, and be careful not to snag it, although a lot of distortion can be corrected off the loom by pulling gently on the bias. Use firm tension and a gentle beat while weaving.

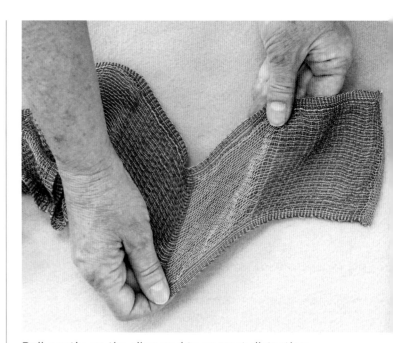

Pull gently on the diagonal to correct distortion.

PROJECT DETAILS

Four-color scarf with six color variations

Pattern/Structure: Open tubular double weave with single-layer selvedges and hems for the 6-shaft version, open tubular double weave with single-layer hems for the 4-shaft version.

Warp: 20/2 pearl cotton at 8,400 yd. (7,681 m)/ lb. from Lunatic Fringe in two colors, 5 Yellow and 5 Yellow Red.

Warp width: Approx. 5 in. (12.7 cm) (104 ends)

Warp length: 3 yd. (2.7 m)

Sett: 40 e.p.i. for the selvedges (either version), 10 e.p.i. for each of the double-weave layers (20 e.p.i. overall). Use a 10-dent reed, sleying selvedges 4 per dent and the center 4 in. (10.2 cm) at 2 per dent.

Picks per inch (2.5 cm): 40 for hems, 10 per layer for open-weave areas

Use floating selvedges and two shuttles.

Weft: 20/2 pearl cotton from Lunatic Fringe in two colors, 10 Blue and 10 Green.

Picks per inch: Approx. 10 per layer (20 total picks) in the open areas, 40 for the close single layers at the ends.

Take-up: 15% width, 2% length

Total shrinkage: 15% width, 6% length

Finished size: 4¼ in. wide, 68 in. long (10.8 cm wide, 173 cm long)

6-Shaft Version

Wind orange and yellow warps together. Thread the first 12 ends, starting at the right side with orange on shaft 5 and alternating with yellow on shaft 6 (or starting at the left selvedge on shaft 6). Thread the center section, alternating colors as before, on shafts 1 through 4 (repeated 20 times = 80 ends). Finish at the left with 12 ends on shafts 5 and 6.

The warps on shafts 5 and 6 are sleyed 4 per dent. The center is sleyed with orange and yellow warps in the same dent, one pair per dent.

Treadles 1 and 10 weave a single layer of plain weave for the ends of the scarf. Treadles 2 through 5 put the orange warps in the top layer; treadles 6 through 9 put the yellow warps on top.

Start both wefts from the same side, leaving a "tail" of one for overcasting. Weave an inch (2.5 cm) of single-layer plain weave, alternating wefts.

Although the hem is woven at 40 picks per inch, it takes a very light beat because of the open sett. As you advance the warp, place a terrycloth towel between the scarf fabric and the breast beam and another around the cloth beam; the nap should smooth down in the direction of the castle. The loops in the towel fill in the open spaces and reduce distortion. Don't worry if there is some distortion; this is easy to correct off the loom.

Weave 4-inch (10.2 cm) sections of each variation, following the treadling sequence. The top-layer warps exchange places with each section. Start each new section with the weft you did not use on top in the previous section.

For sections 1, 2, 4, and 5, weave one color only in the top layer and the other only in the bottom. Beat only after placing the wefts in both layers. Weave a pick in each layer (alternating colors), close the shed, and use the beater very gently to position the two wefts together, maintaining an open balanced weave. The selvedges will be denser. Because there are relatively few points of interlacement, there is little take-up in the open-weave center, and you can weave almost straight across, with just a slight angle or arc. With the shed closed, you can tug the pair of wefts gently to straighten out any little wiggles, on the side where the shuttles just exited.

Sections 3 and 6 use the same color for each pair of weft shots (top and bottom) and alternate the colors for the next picks. Again, beat only after weaving both top and bottom picks.

Section 1: Orange warps on the top layer, yellow on the bottom; weave the blue weft for top-layer picks and the green only on the bottom, changing treadles with each color. Treadles 2 and 4 weave the top layer, alternating with treadles 3 and 5 on the bottom. Weave a pick in each layer before using the beater very gently to position the wefts.

Section 2: Yellow warps are on top, and the green weft weaves the top layer, blue on the bottom.

Section 3: Orange warps are up. Weave top and bottom layers with the same color, then switch colors for the next top and bottom picks: top blue, bottom blue, top green, bottom green. Both weft colors show on each side of the fabric, creating alternate stripes.

Section 4: Yellow warps up; blue on top, green on the bottom.

Section 5: Orange warps up; green on top, blue on the bottom.

Section 6: Similar to section 3, but with yellow warps on top.

Weave the 6-section sequence three times, then weave a close single layer for 1 inch (2.5 cm), alternating wefts. Loosely overcast the edge and cut the scarf from the loom. Serge or zigzag the cut ends, turn them under twice and stitch, to form narrow rolled hems.

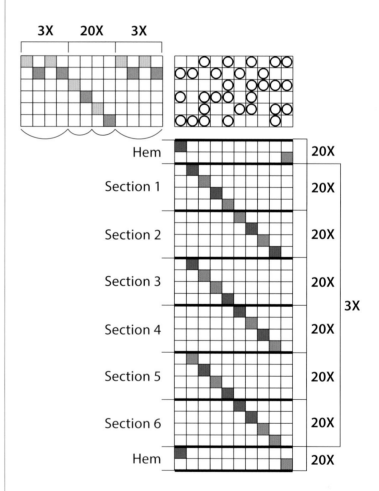

= in the same dent

4-Shaft Version

Weaving and color sequences are the same, but you will probably need to use a skeleton tie-up and treadle with both feet when weaving the bottom layers, if you are using a 4-shaft floor loom.

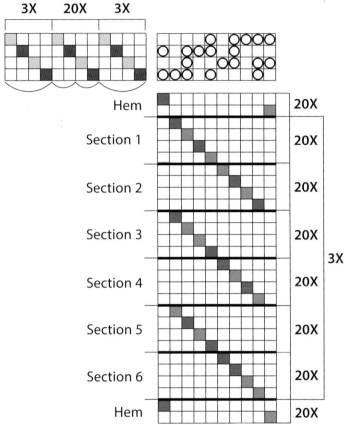

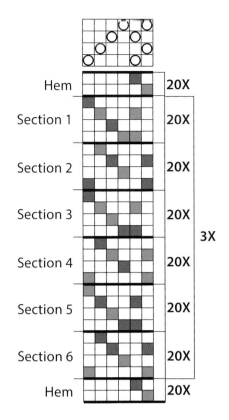

skeleton tie-up and treadling

⌣ = in the same dent

Three Scarves on One Warp

These 4-shaft scarves will give you experience with three- and four-color effects, using variations of the French technique. With alternating warp colors functioning as pairs, you can weave with a single shuttle or two for different results. The lustrous Tencel yarn makes fabric that glows with iridescence. Since this is a relatively heavy yarn, the multicolored effect is not as uniform as it would be with finer yarns at a closer sett.

If you prefer to weave just one scarf at a time, use a three-yard (2.7 m) warp for each. Otherwise, this eight-yard (7.3 m) warp is adequate for three fringed scarves.

Wind both warp colors together and thread in pairs on the same shaft but in separate heddles (shafts 1-1, 2-2, 3-3, 4-4), alternating colors. Sley the first end in a dent by itself, then two per dent across the warp, never putting two ends on the same shaft in the same dent (see page 43).

PROJECT DETAILS

Shafts required: 4

Pattern/Structure: Variations of half-basketweave (doubled weft in plain weave) and basketweave with warps and wefts with twill treadlings

Warp width: 6 in. (15.2 cm) (180 ends)

Warp length: 8 yd. (7.32 m) for 3 fringed scarves, each 2 yd. (1.8 m) long with 8 in. (20.3 cm) of fringe on each end

Sett: 30 e.p.i., 3/dent in a 10-dent reed or 2-3 in a 12-dent reed

Picks per inch (2.5 cm): Varies; see individual instructions

Warp: 8/2 Tencel at 3,360 yd. (3,072 m)/lb., from Webs; allow 4 oz. (113.4 g) each of New Red and Gold.

Wefts: 8/2 Tencel at 3,360 yd. (3,072 m)/lb. from Webs; allow 4 oz. (113.4 g) each of Aquamarine and Iris.

Take-up: Approx. 11% width, 3% length

Total shrinkage:
Three-Color Scarf in Half-Basketweave, 21% width, 6% length

Four-Color Twill Scarf, 12% width, 8% length

Four-Color Scarf with Clasped Wefts, 17% width, 8% length

Finished scarves measure (not including 6 in. [15.2 cm] fringe):
Three-Color Scarf in Half-Basketweave, 4¾ in. (12.1 cm) wide, 68 in. (173 cm) long

Four-Color Twill Scarf, 5¼ in. (13.3 cm) wide, 66 in. (167.6 cm) long

Four-Color Scarf with Clasped Wefts, 5 in. (12.7 cm) wide, 66½ in. (168.9 cm) long

Three-Color Scarf in Half-Basketweave

The first scarf uses a single shuttle and one weft color (aquamarine), and it weaves up quickly in plain weave. I used a gentle beat and about 20 picks per inch (2.5 cm). The structure is half-basketweave. Allow 8 inches (20.3 cm) of warp as fringe at the start, filling at least the last 2 inches (5.1 cm) with a heavy yarn to spread the warp. Any unwoven warp at the start without filler should be packed as it travels around the cloth beam (I used cardboard tubes slit lengthwise).

Leave a "tail" of aquamarine weft three times the width of the warp at the start, and hemstitch after weaving several picks in plain weave. Weave 72 inches (1.8 m) and hemstitch at the end with the weft. Allow 16 inches (40.6 cm) for fringe between scarves, and use filler for at least a couple inches before starting the next scarf. Again, any unwoven sections of warp must have packing around the cloth beam to prevent uneven tension.

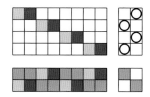

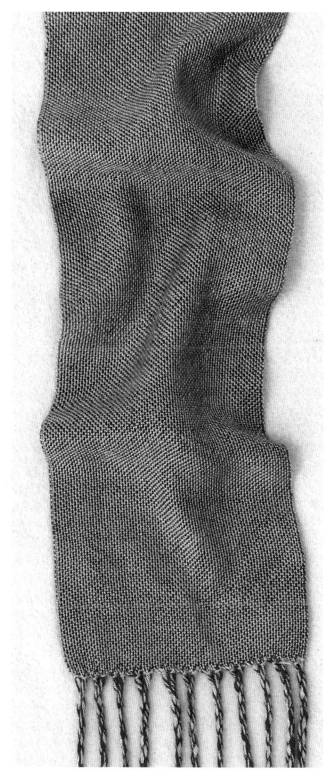

Three-color scarf in half-basketweave

Four-Color Twill Scarf

The second scarf, with both paired warps and wefts, is woven in 2/2 twill and requires a very gentle beat, just using the beater to gently place the wefts. Firm tension helps maintain a light beat; my scarf has about 20 doubled picks per inch (2.5 cm), so is somewhat weft-dominant but still allows the warps to show. This scarf requires two shuttles and each pick must contain both weft colors, which cannot be allowed to cross. The darker weft is difficult to see while you are weaving, yet the finished fabric will show both weft colors as well as both warps.

Floating selvedges are optional and not needed if the shuttles for the first pick (raising shafts 1 and 2) travel toward the selvedge threaded on shaft 1. If adding floating selvedges, maintain the warp color alternation at the sides so you don't end up with two warps of the same color together. Shuttles should travel in the same direction in the same pick. Use the same color sequence for every pick (aquamarine, then iris). To keep the wefts from crossing, it's best to throw the first weft, close the shed and beat, then reopen the same shed and repeat with the second color. You may experiment with throwing both shuttles and beating the wefts together, always beating on a closed shed. The wefts may have a tendency to cross where they enter the shed together, and realigning them takes about as much time as beating them separately.

Hemstitch the edge with the aquamarine weft. Weave 72 inches (1.8 m), hemstitch with the iris weft, and leave 16 inches (40.6 cm) of warp for fringe between this scarf and the third. Again, use a header for at least the last few inches, and be sure to pack any unwoven fringe as it travels around the cloth beam.

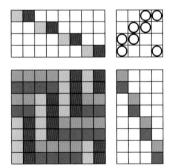

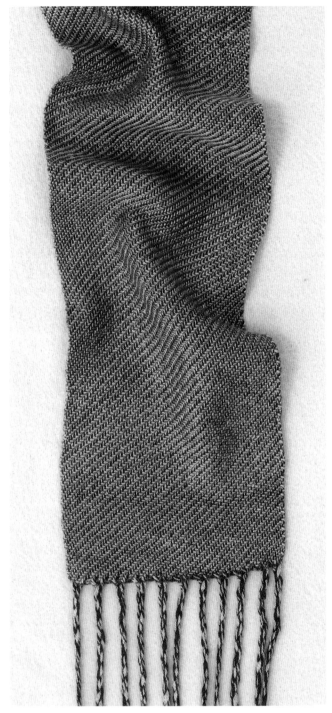

Four-color twill scarf

Four-Color Scarf with Clasped Wefts

The third scarf, using a crêpe (broken twill) treadling and clasped-weft technique, has three colors at each thread intersection. The treadling includes both 2/2 twill and plain weave picks (if it were threaded to the same pattern, true plain weave would not be possible, and the overall pattern would look different). This treadling and the slight bulk of the weft join make it easy to maintain a balanced weave of 14 to 15 doubled picks per inch (2.5 cm), as long as you beat gently.

Clasped-weft technique uses a single shuttle with one weft, which always starts through a shed from the same direction (here, left to right). The shuttle exits the shed and wraps around a strand of the second weft, which remains stationary, usually on a cone or ball. (Here, since I already had the second weft on a shuttle I used for the previous scarf, I left it on the shuttle, but kept the shuttle stationary.)

The working shuttle (I used the aquamarine weft) reenters the *same* shed, right to left, and pulls a loop of the second weft with it. You can position the join anywhere you wish in the shed before you beat. Both wefts are doubled, so the structure is similar to basketweave but with a broken twill treadling.

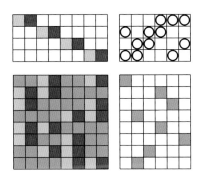

The yarn on the shuttle pulls in a loop of the second (stationary) weft.

Four-color scarf with clasped wefts

For the first pick, pull in enough of the second weft (doubled) so you can tuck its tail into the next shed, or use it to do the hemstitching. (You can hemstitch with either weft.)

Floating selvedges are optional, and most of these wefts will wrap the selvedges without them. I used a floating selvedge only on the side where the working shuttle enters the shed (here, on the left, in gold). A floating selvedge on the other side is a hindrance when the shuttle reenters the shed. (In order to pull in the loop of the second weft, the shuttle would have to go under or over the floater in the same manner as when it exited and would not wrap around it anyway.)

Weave for 72 inches (1.8 m), hemstitch with either weft, and allow at least 8 inches (20.3 cm) for fringe at the end of the warp.

Finishing

Twist the fringe before you wet-finish the fabric, then wash by hand or machine with a mild cleanser. Hang to dry or machine dry. Trim fringe as needed.

Vest Fabric in Double Weave

Although close double weave did not prove appropriate for a drapable scarf (see page 51), this 8-shaft project is well suited for a vest fabric. This yardage should be ample for a woman's large waist-length vest, and you can change the width and alter the length to fit your desired pattern. Because of the block design, you may wish to choose a boxy vest pattern instead of one with curved front panels.

Lay out your pattern to determine the actual width and yardage you need, remembering to add extra to allow for take-up and shrinkage and for matching blocks at seams. You can adapt this pattern to make your blocks smaller or of varying widths by changing the number of threading repeats in a block.

These three-inch (7.6 cm) blocks show off the iridescence well. Each of the two blocks consists of the same two colors throughout, yet depending on the angle of view, they appear to change color from blue to green. At certain angles and some distance, the blocks almost seem to disappear, and color mixing makes the fabric appear blue-green.

Because of the dense sett, this project requires a considerable number of heddles, 180 on each of eight shafts. Thread three inches (7.6 cm) of each block and alternate blocks A and B across the warp. I've chosen Jennifer Moore's innovative and sensible threading and treadling (Jennifer Moore, *Doubleweave*, Interweave, 2010), rather than the more conventional threading used in the double-weave scarf project. The colors can be wound together on a warping board or reel, and they alternate throughout the threading, green on shafts 1, 2, 5, and 6 and blue on shafts 3, 4, 7, and 8. Two shuttles are required. Loosely overcast edges with the weft to secure the ends temporarily.

Weave this fabric under firm, even tension. The weft color order remains constant throughout, even when changing treadling blocks. Start the shuttles at the same side, beat after each pick, and weave each block for three inches (block A uses treadles 1 through 4, block B, treadles 5 through 8). You may occasionally need to use the beater to help clear sheds, especially when changing treadling blocks. Beat firmly after every pick. Be sure the wefts wrap each other at the selvedges, and check occasionally to make sure the edges are joined rather than separate layers. The wrapping varies with the block you are treadling and the side where both shuttles are exiting.

Overcast the end, make any needed corrections, and serge or zigzag the ends. Hem them by turning under ¼ inch (.6 cm) twice. Machine wash in warm water with mild detergent or other cleanser, machine dry until damp, press while damp.

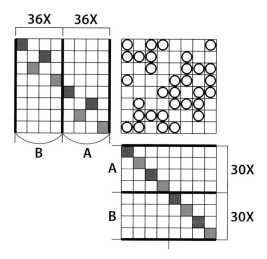

= in the same dent

Pattern: Two-block double weave, 8 shafts
Warp width: 1,440 ends, 30 in. (76.2 cm)
Warp length: 3 yd. (2.7 m)
Sett: 24 e.p.i. per layer (48 e.p.i. overall), 4 per dent in a 12-dent reed
Picks per inch (2.5 cm): 20-22 (a slightly unbalanced weave)
Warp: 10/2 pearl cotton in two colors, approx. 9 oz. (255 g) each of #125 Pacific Blue and #13 Sapphire (green) from UKI/Supreme Corporation
Weft: 10/2 pearl cotton, same colors and amounts as the warp
Take-up: 4% width, 4% length
Total shrinkage: 9% width, 12% length
Finished fabric measurements: 27¼ in. wide, 2 yd., 4 in. long (69.2 cm wide, 1.9 m long)

PROJECT DETAILS

Huck Yardage

This lightweight fabric from fine yarn will make a very comfortable blouse or shirt that's easy to care for. Because it's mostly plain weave, the weaving is easy and relatively fast. Since these colors are closely related, the iridescence is subtle. The red-violet warp cools the intensely warm red slightly while maintaining the overall warmth of the bright colors. The huck spots themselves don't shift color and are not iridescent. However, they form a nice textural accent on the iridescent background. When the background looks mostly magenta, the red floats appear more noticeable, and when the background looks red, you notice the red-violet warp floats.

You should be able to weave at least four yards (3.7 m) of fabric, and three yards (2.7 m) of finished (washed) fabric is plenty for many commercial patterns, allowing some leeway to bypass any flaws.

At this width and sett, this project requires a lot of heddles, especially on shafts 1 and 4. You may be able to reduce the width or use heavier threads for a vest or jacket fabric instead, or use a loom with more shafts and adjust the draft to put some of the threads on higher shafts. As I usually do with fine yarns and a wide warp, I used a temple (stretcher) for this fabric, placed just inside the breast beam, where it was not in danger of scratching the shuttlerace. I only moved it when I advanced the warp, and it still reduced draw-in and shrinkage and eliminated selvedge breakage.

Start weaving with two inches (5.1 cm) of plain weave and overcast the edge.

Use firm tension and a moderate beat, slightly lighter for the lace picks, with 22 picks of plain weave between the lace sections (not including the plain weave picks that start and end the lace blocks). From the start of one lace block to the start of the next should be approximately an inch (2.5 cm).

End with two inches (5.1 cm) of plain weave, and overcast the edge as you did at the start. Off the loom, make any needed corrections, serge or zigzag the edges, and make a narrow rolled hem on each end (turning under ¼ inch [.6 cm] twice) before machine washing the fabric in warm water with a little detergent or mild soap. Machine dry, warm; press the fabric while slightly damp.

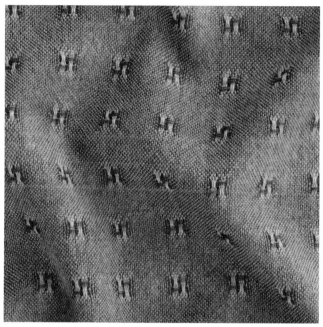

This alternate colorway using 5 Red Purple for the warp and 10 Blue as the weft creates a cooler fabric. The same red-violet warp warms the royal blue, and because the colors are not as closely related, the iridescence is more noticeable.

PROJECT DETAILS

Pattern: Huck, turned spots, 4 shafts (adapted from pattern V9C by Helene Bress, *The Weaving Book*, Charles Scribner's Sons, 1981)

Warp width: 1,026 ends, approx. 32 in. (81.3 cm)

Warp length: 5 yd. (4.6 m)

Sett: 32 e.p.i., sleyed 2-3-3 in a 12-dent reed

Picks per inch (2.5 cm): Approx. 40

Warp: 9.9 oz. (280.7 g) of 20/2 pearl cotton at 8,400 yd. (7,681 m)/lb., 5 Red Purple from Lunatic Fringe

Weft: 6.25 oz. (177.2 g) of 20/2 pearl cotton, 10 Red from Lunatic Fringe (I used an additional 1.1 oz. [31.2 g] for extra yardage)

Take-up: 5% width, 11% length

Total shrinkage: 8% width, 16% length

Finished fabric measurements: 29½ in. wide, 3 yd. for the 4-yd. length (measured on the loom under tension) (74.9 cm wide, 2.7 m for the 3.7 m length)

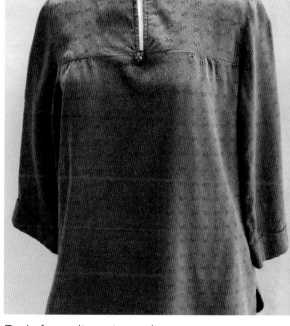

Tunic from alternate yardage.

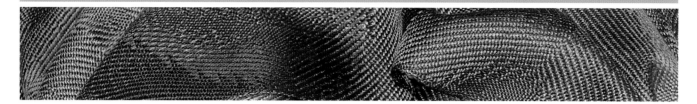

The thought of tackling the photography was a reason I delayed writing this book for a number of years. Iridescent fabrics respond best to movement, and creating still images that will exhibit color changes is a major challenge. While a professional photographer might have had better equipment and skills, most professionals in my region are unaccustomed to working with textiles, and I felt the need to be present during the process.

In order to show the cloth at different angles in one picture, it helps to drape or crumple the fabric; soft folds accenting both warp and weft allow you to see the color changes that happen at different angles of view. Photos of multicolored fabrics need to show color changes in more than two directions. I became somewhat adept at "artful crumpling," the same technique I request when sending off weavings for exhibit (accompanied by a snapshot of how I'd like a piece displayed).

Photographing iridescent fabrics in sunlight or with flash can accentuate the colors, but those conditions (particularly bright sunlight) can also create dark shadows that mask some colors. We chose to use diffused natural light and a neutral (50 percent gray) felt background for most shots, photographing the pieces horizontally and using a tripod. A few shots worked better in bright light or taken at an angle to better show off component colors or patterns. Even in diffused light, brilliantly lustrous fabrics sometimes reflected so much light that parts of them look white in the photos. Fabrics that combine both lustrous and dull threads were also challenging.

The color-changing fabric shown on pages 54–55 was photographed in bright sunlight with a cover over half the fabric. The mask was removed just before the shutter clicked and before the sun could color that half of the sample.

Digital cameras seem particularly good at managing depth of field, even when the fabrics are crumpled so that they require good focus at different distances from the lens. They have made photography faster and easier in many ways, but they are not as adept as the human eye at identifying nuances of color, partly because of the correction features built into them. We used automatic settings for most of the photos. However, black and other very dark fabrics do not reproduce well that way; on an automatic setting, the camera tries to correct black to gray, producing unsatisfactory results. (However, the pleated black-and-white fabrics photographed well, maybe because the camera decided the white averaged with the black was the equivalent of gray.) One very dark but relatively sheer fabric, lacking any luster and crossing blue and green of the same value, refused to cooperate with the camera (or vice versa), and was not included in this book. Red fabric is also problematic; the color overpowers less brilliant colors and even masks textural details. These special challenges required manual settings (as well as some color correction on the computer) for best results.

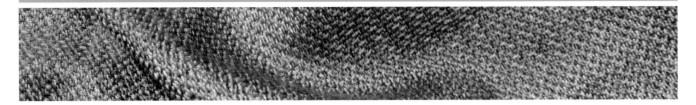

The following references have been particularly useful to me in understanding various aspects of the topics in this book.

Cuin, David E. *Take Control of Color: Creating Drama and Impact in Arts and Crafts.* Dectra Corp., 2013. ISBN 978-0-9883-7480-5.

Written by an artist primarily for painters, this book is a useful guide to color theory that makes brief reference to textile arts.

Falk, David S., Dieter R. Brill, and David G. Stork. *Seeing the Light: Optics in Nature, Photography, Color, Vision, and Holography.* John Wiley & Sons, 1986. ISBN 978-0-4716-0385-6.

This book for nonphysicists makes sense of very technical topics in a manner that's not only easy to read and understand, but also entertaining.

Lambert, Patricia, Barbara Staepelaere, and Mary G. Fry. *Color and Fiber.* Schiffer, 1986. ISBN 0-88740-065-5.

Iridescence is only a minor topic in this book, emphasizing multicolored effects and mostly in relation to stitching images of natural objects. There is only scant reference to weaving iridescent fabrics. However, this book is a good resource for understanding optical effects, color systems, and color theory as related to yarn and textiles.

Menz, Deb. *ColorWorks: The Crafter's Guide to Color.* Interweave Press, 2004. ISBN 978-1-9314-9947-7.

Easy to understand, this is one of few books with a focus on color in textiles and fibers, including spinning, knitting, weaving, embroidery, surface design, quilting, and paper collage. It includes numerous removable color reference charts, including gray-scale guides.

Stubenitsky, Marian. *Weaving with Echo and Iris.* Self-published; 2013–2014. English version translated by Margreet Ward, 2014. ISBN 978-90-822182-0-6.

The author presents her results from many years of study and teaching using primarily echo weave and double weave to achieve very colorful woven fabrics, including some iridescent in multiple colors. Projects range from 4 shafts to 32.